MW01231629

"This is an extremely ~~useful introduction~~
of the Bible. Whether someone is new to the faith or has been
a Christian for several years, *Sketchy Views* is an introduction
to theology that will support spiritual growth and knowledge
of the Bible."

Melissa Tucker, Professor of Teacher Education,
Boyce College

"Daniel DeWitt illustrates his message with words, stories,
and even sketches to make this helpful book accessible and
memorable. No matter where you're at in your spiritual journey, *Sketchy Views* will encourage, challenge, and assist you in
thinking biblically about God."

Jeff Dalrymple, Executive Director, the Evangelical
Council for Abuse Prevention

"There's no shortage of books today telling us what to think
about God. So why pick up this book? Because in a forest filled
with pathways, what we need most are wise and experienced
guides. Daniel DeWitt is such a guide. In this book, Daniel
shows us how to find and traverse the trail of thought that
leads to a discovery of God. I'm delighted to recommend this
book by a guide I trust."

T. J. Tims, Lead Pastor, Immanuel Church, Nashville, TN

"In typical Daniel DeWitt fashion, this book successfully takes
thinkers on an epic journey into the most important topic
they could consider: God. Mixing ample cultural allusions
with a healthy dose of humor (sometimes self-deprecating,
sometimes merely dad jokes, but always keeping the reader
on task), DeWitt guides his readers through some of the most
treacherous theological waters they will ever face."

Jonathan Arnold, Associate Professor of Theological
Studies, Cedarville University

"What we believe about God our Creator is the most important thing about us. It shapes how we live in the world. It impacts how we serve our family, friends, and neighbors. It matters for both this life and eternity. That's why *Sketchy Views* is a great resource for Christians to think about what they believe."

FLAME, Grammy-nominated and Stellar award-winning artist

"Daniel DeWitt is a friendly and trusted guide to help us come to terms with what we can know about God and the world he has put us in. This book will be eye-opening for those wanting to think theologically for the first time, and wonderfully refreshing for those who've been doing so for years. It's a pleasure to commend it."

Sam Allberry, Pastor; author

"In a day when sketchy views of God abound, this is a timely resource to help you think clearly and biblically about not only what you believe but why. Daniel DeWitt puts his years of teaching university students and speaking at youth ministry conferences to full use in providing a beginner's guide for making sense of the God of the Bible."

Rick Melson, President, Southwest Baptist University

"Daniel DeWitt's gracious humility, friendly humor, gentle consideration, and easy-to-follow logic make complex concepts surprisingly easy to understand and controversial topics approachable. I look forward to giving *Sketchy Views* to my friends and family."

Jennifer Greenberg, Author of *Not Forsaken: A Story of Life After Abuse*

Sketchy Views

A BEGINNER'S GUIDE
TO MAKING SENSE OF GOD

— DANIEL DEWITT —

New
Growth
Press
newgrowthpress.com

New Growth Press, Greensboro, NC 27401
Copyright © 2023 by Daniel DeWitt
newgrowthpress.com

All rights reserved. No part of this publication may be reproduced, stored in a retrieval system, or transmitted in any form by any means, electronic, mechanical, photocopy, recording, or otherwise, without the prior permission of the publisher, except as provided by USA copyright law.

Unless otherwise indicated, Scripture quotations marked CSB have been taken from the Christian Standard Bible®, Copyright © 2017 by Holman Bible Publishers. Used by permission. Christian Standard Bible® and CSB® are federally registered trademarks of Holman Bible Publishers.

Scripture quotations marked ESV have been taken from the ESV® Bible (The Holy Bible, English Standard Version®) copyright © 2001 by Crossway Bibles, a publishing ministry of Good News Publishers. The ESV® text has been reproduced in cooperation with and by permission of Good News Publishers. Unauthorized reproduction of this publication is prohibited. All rights reserved.

Scripture quotations marked HCSB have been taken from the Holman Christian Standard Bible®, Copyright © 1999, 2000, 2002, 2003, 2009 by Holman Bible Publishers. Used by permission.

Scripture quotations marked NIV are taken from the Holy Bible, New International Version®, NIV®. Copyright © 1973, 1978, 1984, 2011 by Biblica, Inc.™ Used by permission of Zondervan. All rights reserved worldwide. www.zondervan.com. The "NIV" and "New International Version" are trademarks registered in the United States Patent and Trademark Office by Biblica, Inc.™

Cover Design: Facout Studio, faceoutstudio.com
Interior Typesetting and eBook: Lisa Parnell

ISBN: 978-1-64507-288-1 (Print)
ISBN: 978-1-64507-289-8 (eBook)

Library of Congress Cataloging-in-Publication Data on file

Printed in the United States of America

30 29 28 27 26 25 24 23   1 2 3 4 5

To Wendol and Nancy Eaton,

two of the finest people I know, whom my children are blessed to call Papaw and Mamaw.

Contents

A Stream Called Orthodoxy

*To complain that man measures God by his own experience
is a waste of time; man measures everything by his own
experience; he has no other yardstick.*
—DOROTHY L. SAYERS

The river looked like fire. The red beams of the rising sun reflected off the water, cutting through the fog hanging in the tree-lined banks. Steam lofted upward like smoke, releasing yesterday's heat.

As I put my kayak in the water for a morning of fishing, my thoughts turned to God.

Nature has always had that effect on me. There's something primordial, biblical even, about the way nature points beyond itself. For me, the call of the wild has always been an invitation to think deeply about God.

What comes to mind when you think about God? Your answer reveals one of the most important things about you.[1] It reveals your *theology*, the term we use to describe how we organize our thoughts about God. This will touch nearly every area of your life.

Theology literally means "words about God." Because God is the most important topic a person can think about, the way we view him—our theology—is the most valuable and important collection of our thoughts and words. Every person is a theologian because every person has some sort of opinion about God.

Even atheism is a theological position since it's a belief about God—a belief that God doesn't exist. Atheism can't be proven. It's accepted on faith. It too is a theology, the sketchiest of all views of God.

This book is a beginner's guide to making sense of theology—of God. If you haven't thought about theology much before, why not start now? If you've already given it a lot of time and energy, why not keep going? Wherever you are in your spiritual journey, I hope this book can spur you on in your thoughts about God. But first, back to fishing. (Don't worry, this isn't a book about fishing. But you should probably know, I love to fish. So it might come up on occasion.)

Looking for God

My family and I live in central Ohio, in an area surrounded by streams. Since I grew up fishing in farm ponds and small lakes in the flatlands of Illinois, I've had to learn some new techniques. Fishing in streams is a different ball game.

Splashing around in a stony creek on a midsummer day feels glorious. (Even if you don't like to fish, I bet you'd enjoy the experience.) The cool water gurgling its way around boulders and bends. The sun peeking through the veil of leafy branches overhead. The pools of still water resting behind large rocks and in the broad flats. The birds singing in the trees. The deer shyly crossing the creek up ahead. This is my kind of therapy.

When you're fishing in a stream, it's important which way you face. Fish have a limited amount of energy to eat a maximum number of calories. Fish are hunters, and they know how to find a good meal. They aren't going to fight the rapids all day long. They're going to make their way to optimal hunting grounds, situate themselves in a nice spot where they aren't constantly swimming against the current, and wait for food to come to them. That means they'll be lurking in certain kinds of places, looking in a specific direction.

They wait. The water will bring them their entrée. Maybe the current will deliver a bug or a worm or a fly. They'll sit patiently, seemingly frozen in the water, with the exception of small movements of their tail. It's almost like a dog waiting for you to put food in their bowl, until finally dinner is served. When the fish see what they want, they're going to strike. If it's a largemouth bass, they might even jump out of the water like a great white on Shark Week. The whole thing is pretty exhilarating in my humble but accurate opinion.

Where to Look

When it comes to thinking about God, it's important to look in the right direction too. That doesn't mean you can't learn anything about God from looking in other directions. I'm just saying that where you start organizing your thoughts about God is foundational. Here's what I mean.

Looking to experience

As one option, you could make your own life experience your focal point for thinking about God. That's what most people do. I've certainly done that before too. We could think about life or about our experiences. Then ask something like, what must God be like?

This is an understandable place to begin. We can't help but see God through the lens of our lives. As Dorothy Sayers said in the quote at the beginning of this chapter, we have no other yardstick by which to measure. We see the world through the lenses of our past experiences.

As it has been said, there is no view from nowhere. We are all standing somewhere, and wherever we're standing will tend to shape our perspective. Your location frames your outlook.

Have you ever had a bad seat at a concert or movie that made it difficult to see the show? You couldn't see over the tall person with a hat sitting in front of you or around a post. Or worst of all, maybe you got stuck in the front row and ended up with an insufferable neck cramp. Annoying, isn't it? Where you sit can make a big difference in how you experience what you see.

The same is true in how we think about God. Wherever we're from or living now, whatever our circumstances in life have been, they all affect our view of God. Maybe you're from a broken family like me. That can affect your view of God. Our experiences can be like sunglasses, coloring everything we look at.

This isn't always a bad thing. On the one hand, good experiences can have a good effect. For example, maybe you have a great relationship with your dad. He's loving and patient and enjoys spending time with you. That can shape your view of your Heavenly Father in a positive way. But it may not take you long to think of ways your experiences can shape your beliefs in unhelpful ways. Even positive experiences can blind us to reality.

For instance, some might see their success in life as a sign that God is good with everything they do. But what if he isn't? On the other hand, people who are sensitive to their own shortcomings or failures might see God as an unaccepting, angry judge who's sick and tired of dealing with all their mess-ups. They feel they're one mistake away from being kicked out for good. Maybe that's how you see

God. But that's not the way the Bible talks about God. That means you need to recalibrate your feelings around the facts.

There are ditches on both sides of this road. Whether positive or negative, we need to interpret our experiences in light of what's true and not just based on our feelings at any particular moment. We need to find a way to see things more objectively than our subjective experience.

Looking to nature

Another place people look to make sense of God is creation. That's not an entirely bad idea either. After all, one way to learn something about an artist is to look at their art. If God made the world, then perhaps the world can tell us something about its Creator. As I've mentioned, I love spending time in creation. It makes me think of God. But is nature the best place to begin our theology?

The idea of the natural world pointing to God is actually found in the Bible. King David says the heavens declare the glory of God (Psalm 19:1). The apostle Paul says creation reveals God's invisible attributes (Romans 1:20). So, according to the Bible, we can know something about God from creation. But the questions are, how much can we learn about God from creation, and is our experience in nature the best starting point for trying to make sense of God?

We often take the sum total of our understanding of the world and make it foundational for how we make sense of God. For example, some take the scientific consensus of the moment and make it the rule by which they measure Scripture. After all, the biblical authors were living in the same physical universe we are today. So, while our study of the world can at times inform how we read a biblical text, we can't make scientific consensus supreme in our biblical interpretation.

At times, something we learn about nature helps us understand what a biblical author is describing. For example, when David talks about the rising and setting of the sun in Psalm 19, we know he was using language to express his point of view. To him, as it is to us, it seems as though the sun is rising and setting. It's really not.

Through a study of the natural world, we can understand the earth's orbit and know it only appears that the sun is moving around the earth. David is no more wrong in describing the sun in the Psalms than a meteorologist is for announcing the time of the sunrise.

While these insights are helpful, we're heading toward a sketchy view of God if we make science the gatekeeper for our beliefs about him. As Christians we believe in a supernatural God who is beyond nature, who is able to interact with nature in powerful ways that defy our scientific categories. As created beings, we can't make ourselves or the creation the standard for understanding the Creator.

Looking to the mind

Still another view would be to measure everything by our own intellect. If something in the Bible doesn't make sense to us, we can discount it or ignore it. When we treat God's Word in this way, we're really making our brain the ultimate authority, instead of the Bible.

Don't get me wrong; I think the intellectual life is really important. Ignorance is not a virtue, and poor understanding and bad arguments aren't a model for the Christian life. But there are things about God that we just can't grasp— that go well beyond our intellectual reasoning. So, while we want to grow in our knowledge of who God is, we don't want to make our mental ability the real master and the Bible the servant. That's the exact opposite of how we should frame our theology.

A long time ago in a land far away there was a philosopher named Protagoras. He believed humans are the measure for all things, determining what's real, what exists, and what doesn't. There was someone long before him who taught that too. He showed up as a snake in the garden of Eden. Making ourselves the authority for what God is like and how to relate to him is a sketchy view as old as the third chapter in Genesis.

Facing the Wrong Direction

None of us like what psychologists call "cognitive dissonance." That's when we believe something that doesn't quite line up with the world around us. Let's say you trust a close friend, but you keep hearing that they are saying negative things about you behind your back. You believe them to be trustworthy, but your experience is pointing in the opposite direction. When we face challenges to our beliefs like these, we will often begin exploring new beliefs to better explain the situation.

Is that how we should handle our theology? If our beliefs hit troubled waters, should we begin editing our convictions to accommodate our experience? It's certainly hard to avoid this. But is this the best way to make sense of God?

Have you ever thought, *I wouldn't believe in a God like that*? I know I have. Maybe something you read in the Bible is difficult to understand or accept. It just doesn't line up with a common sense view of things. What should we do? Reject what the Bible says or reject our feelings?

Let me ask another question: What if God is different than we expect? What if he doesn't line up with all our experiences or expectations? What if we're looking in the wrong direction when we're thinking about God? What then? What now?

If something seems clear in Scripture but goes against our intellect, our understanding of nature, or our own personal experience, we might dismiss it or assume the Bible is saying something other than what it is. When we do this, we allow our experiences in the world to retrofit the Bible. We make ourselves the authority over what God has said about himself. In forming our theology this way, we shape our view of God based on our own lives and then find a way to make Scripture conform.

God in the Mirror?

Here's the problem with this method: we end up with a God who looks a lot like our experiences, a lot like the person who stares back at us from the mirror—a God who looks like us. I remember hearing a Christian leader once say something like, God made us in his image, and he didn't ask us to return the favor. If we make our experience in the world our starting point and authority, we'll end up custom making a God to our own specifications, one who never challenges our assumptions, aspirations, or appetites.

The Bible describes this as idolatry. If we make a god in our own image, after our own preferences, we've merely made an idol. If what you think about God is one of the most important things about you, then the last thing you want is to feel right but be dead wrong.

It's easy to gravitate toward sketchy views that better fit with how we want to live than to begin and end with Scripture. There are about a million ways to get God wrong. There's a narrow path to getting God right. Making our lives or the world the chief authority for forming important beliefs is the path to sketchy views of God. The **goal of this book** is to point you in the right direction in your lifelong quest to form proper beliefs about God. This is what Christians for centuries have described as *orthodoxy*.

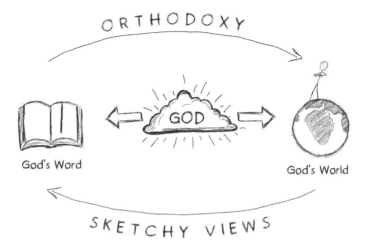

Drawing Straight Lines

Followers of Jesus have often used two different terms—*orthodoxy* and *heresy*—to distinguish between acceptable and unacceptable views of God. *Orthodoxy* means acquiring rightly ordered or formed beliefs about God, in the same way an orthodontist wants to straighten your teeth.

Heresy, on the other hand, means getting God wrong. The British theologian Alister McGrath points out the "essential feature of a heresy is that it is not unbelief." Heresy is a poorly formed belief that is unhelpful and destructive. McGrath says heretical beliefs are "subversive or destructive" and thus can indirectly lead to unbelief.[2]

Throughout this book, when I use the term *sketchy views*, I'm really talking about heresy. Heresy doesn't flow from or fit with the text of Scripture. These are beliefs that don't line up with the way Christians have interpreted the Bible for the last two thousand years. They might be beliefs that fit a particular mood or experience, but they aren't lined up with how Christians have historically made sense of what God has revealed about himself in Scripture.

People who promote sketchy views of God are often called *heretics*. I regularly tell students in my theology courses that one of my main goals for them is that they not become heretics. That's one of my goals for you as well. It's a simple goal, but it can be far more difficult than it sounds. Heresy is subtle and seductive.

So I'll just state it up front: don't become a heretic. Don't develop sketchy views of God that don't line up with the Bible. The goal of the book is to point you in the right direction. This is more of a beginner's guide because there are a lot of things I could say, or would like to say, but can't. I'm going to introduce you to some big topics—to sketch the outline of biblical truth in broad strokes. I will begin with a bit of an overview, then model for you how to get started in the right way.

Facing the Right Direction

Just like that hungry fish looking for a meal upstream, it's important to know which way to look when we think about God. It's been said there are three good starting places for making sense of God. First, there is **human reason**. God made you in his image as a thinking being. You have a brain. When it's working properly, it can direct you to truth. In fact, one of my favorite definitions of faith is "well-reasoned trust." Our brains are tools we can use in our understanding of God.

Though reason can play an important role in our relationship with God, it can only take us so far. We can have good reasons to believe in God. But true faith follows our reason where it leads but then goes beyond where it's able to take us. Reason goes a certain distance in explaining God, but there's so much mystery to who God is, we can't expect reason to bring us all the way. As we mentioned earlier, we have to take the next step beyond where our reason can take us. That's faith.

The second source for thinking about God is church history or what we might call **tradition**. British author G. K. Chesterton said that tradition is "the democracy of the dead."[3] By looking at how Christians over the centuries have thought about the issues, we're giving past believers a vote in how we think about God. We're letting them teach us. This is important, and we'll cover a good deal of it in each chapter.

The truth is, however, that even the best thinkers of the past were still only human. Though they lived long ago and didn't face the same contemporary challenges we do today, they still could get things wrong. They were as susceptible to sketchy views as we are. Nonetheless, we need to give them a voice. We need to let their lives and writings teach us, learning from both their positive and even negative examples. We would be fools not to.

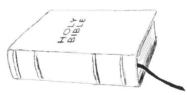

The third source is **Scripture**. Of these three sources, I'm going to make a case throughout the book that the correct starting point is the Bible. Though reason and tradition are important and helpful, they are not supreme. Scripture is the direction in which we need to look. The stream of orthodoxy flows straight from Scripture through our reason and tradition. The best way to avoid sketchy views of God is to begin with the Bible and return to it often.

An Impossible Task?

When we start with Scripture, and not our experiences in the world, we allow it to challenge our assumptions—to interpret our perceptions. Instead of letting our lives define what God must be like, we let God determine what our lives should be like.

Now, there's a problem with what I'm proposing, and some of you may have already thought of it: removing all your experiences is impossible. We're not blank slates. No one approaches the Bible from nowhere. We're all looking toward Scripture from a particular place in time and space.

Authors Randolph Richards and Brandon O' Brien illustrate this challenge in their book *Misreading Scripture with Western Eyes*. They helpfully remind us how we all "tend to read Scripture in our own *when* and *where*, in a way that makes sense on our terms."[4] As they point out, much of what shapes our reading of the Bible is below the surface, things we haven't fully explored, much like the tip of an iceberg.

We all have baggage, and we all bring it to the Bible. This could be something we've been taught or a belief we've formed on our own that doesn't square well with Scripture. If we're not careful, we'll come to the place where we mute, ignore, or deny the parts of the Bible that challenge and don't fit with what we want to be true. Our obstinance in refusing to let the Bible confront and change our views is baggage.

There's baggage we're aware of and baggage we've never really thought about before—what we might call *unexamined* baggage. First, we need to think about our baggage, those assumptions we bring to the Bible. Then we want to examine it in light of the Bible, just like a TSA agent would do with a suspicious suitcase at the airport. Our goal is to have as little unexamined baggage as possible—to be fully aware of things that might keep us from seeing Scripture in all its splendor.

Those who think they are the least affected by this are probably the most blind to their own baggage. So our first step is to hold our baggage lightly. If the Bible challenges our previously formed beliefs or assumptions, we should loosen our grip on those. What will we choose—our baggage or the Bible?

I once had a student who didn't believe in the Trinity. She told me my class was challenging her assumptions and making her go back to Scripture to really figure out what she believes about God. That's a good example of letting the Bible be the authority and holding onto our assumptions loosely.

This is hard work. It's not easy. But it's not as impossible as it might sound.

While we can never fully remove ourselves from our experiences or circumstances, it's possible to be challenged and shaped by the Bible. It will take time. It will take thought. It will take work. But it's worth it. Remember, how you respond to the question of what you think about God is one of the most important things about you.

If you want to develop a biblical way of seeing the world, what we call a biblical worldview, then you need to read the Bible. A lot. The more you immerse yourself in the world of the Bible, in the glorious story of God's saving grace, the more you'll look at the world and your place in it from God's perspective. That's what it means to have a biblical worldview, to see the world through the lens of what God has revealed about himself.

The apostle Paul explains the path to not being conformed to the world is by being transformed by the

renewing of our minds (Romans 12:1–2). Instead of con-
forming the Bible to ourselves, he says we should conform
our lives to it. We should let it transform the way we think
about God, ourselves, and this world we live in. The Bible
describes someone who has experienced a life-changing
encounter with Jesus as a new creation. That means God is
rewriting the believer's life story. But in our desire to do our
own thing, we often try to take the pencil back. We want to
have the final say. And that's when we start sketching out
what we think God should look like. This is where we start
going wrong and develop sketchy views.

Our minds are renewed by being saturated in what
God has revealed about himself, our world, and our lives.
What he said sets our agenda; it frames our beliefs. C. S.
Lewis said something really important that we will return
to throughout the book: "Christians believe God himself
has told us how to speak of him."[5] Orthodoxy begins with
letting God frame our thoughts of how we speak of him. We
can properly see who we are only in relationship to a proper
understanding of who he is. To put it another way, we can
only see ourselves in his light.

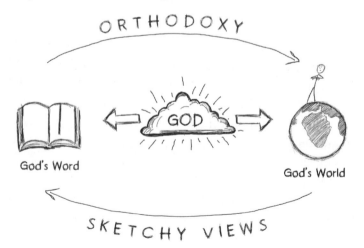

The Mind of God and the Mainstream

When I was a junior in high school, I remember flipping through the famous book *A Brief History of Time*, written by the atheistic scientist Stephen Hawking. I later learned it was described as "the world's least-read bestseller," which means a lot of people bought it, but few read it.

Given its author didn't believe in God, the book ends with a startling quote. Hawking describes his desire to find a scientific theory of the world that can make sense of everything. He says when we discover such a theory, we will know the mind of God.[6] What! Since Hawking didn't believe in God, he obviously wasn't describing some sort of spiritual experience. He meant something like, if we discover a "theory of everything" we'll have solved the mystery of the universe. In other words, we don't need God. We can figure this out ourselves.

I had been a Christian for a little over a year when I read those words. Deep down I knew they were off base. Even then I realized that if we are to know the mind of God, it wouldn't be because we are clever or good. God would have to reveal his mind to us. Our starting point wouldn't be our experience in the world, or even a theory of the entire world. Our starting point would have to be God telling us something about himself. That's precisely what God has done in the Bible. That's where we have to begin. That's where we begin and end. That's where we look.

Sketching Essential Truths

If you've ever kayaked on a stream or gone whitewater rafting with a group, you know there are many tributaries branching off the main body of water. These are always fun to explore. As a fisherman, I rarely pass up an opportunity to get out of the current and see what might be lurking in these distributaries.

When it comes to theology, some truths are mainstream. Then there are some doctrines off the main current like distributaries. We really don't want to leave any terrain uncharted or unexplored, because all the truth in the Bible is from God and intended for our good. Yet there are some doctrines of greater significance when it comes to understanding, ignoring, or rejecting them.

For example, what you believe about end times and Jesus's return is not as important as what you believe about Jesus's death, burial, and resurrection. The view of end times is called *eschatology*, and the view of salvation is called *soteriology*. It's not that eschatology doesn't matter. It does. It just doesn't matter as much as what you believe about how a person is made right with God, or *soteriology*.

As an old theologian once said, "In essentials, unity; in non-essentials, liberty; in all things, charity."[7] In a quick sketch using broad strokes, I'm going to focus on the essential things about the Bible, God, and creation. There are a lot of tributaries we will leave unexamined. Orthodoxy has always been more about the main current, which is where we will spend most of our time.

Some may wish I'd said more on certain topics. Others will wish for less. My goal is not to be overly restrictive. There are areas where Christians will interpret the Bible differently. I firmly believe the stream of orthodoxy is broad enough for all sincere believers to dive into. That's not a baptism pun. Or maybe it is. I am Baptist after all.

Even my poor attempt at humor illustrates my point. Orthodoxy is something all genuine Christians share in, regardless of their particular denomination or the name on their church sign. One of my dearest friends is Anglican. Another close friend is Lutheran. We differ from each other in how we see and explain baptism. Yet I don't feel the need to cut them off, call them heretics, punch them in the nose, or refuse to be friends with them. Christianity is big enough for us to disagree about secondary issues and still get along and work together to advance the gospel.

In issues where I might differ in my theology from other Christians, I certainly want to be charitable. There are more than enough angry-spirited scuffles online between people who profess to be followers of Jesus. I don't want to add noise or heat to debates over nonessential issues. I'm going to resist the temptation to wade into those troubled waters as much as possible.

In this book, I want to survey the depths of three of the biggest areas of theology. We're going to explore God's revelation, the doctrine of God himself, and how we should understand the world we live in. There's a lot more to theology than these three areas, but this is a great place to start in organizing our beliefs about God.

C. S. Lewis used a different metaphor for what I'm talking about. He called his project *Mere Christianity*. He described his goal as seeking to lead people into the main hallway in the house of Christianity. This hallway was meant to illustrate those basic beliefs Christians of all times share in common, providing the basis of their unity. Lewis told his readers that the fireplaces and dining tables, the relationships, and the laughter, were all located in the different rooms of the house. He considered those rooms to be different churches or denominations. While he wanted to introduce readers to the hallway, his goal for them was, in time, to settle into a room. That would be my hope for you as well.

C. S. Lewis's point was not to get people to indefinitely linger in the hallway of *Mere Christianity*. He wanted them to read the Bible and figure out for themselves the room that best represented their specific beliefs. It's inevitable and even desirable for a Christian to move beyond mere Christianity, beyond the fundamental elements of Christian doctrine. Yet, while you will believe more than the basic truths of the Christian faith, you certainly must never believe less. That's the nature of orthodoxy.

A Method for the Mystery

In formulating our theology, it's helpful to have a basic method to think through our thoughts about God. A lot more can go into our approach to theology, but the following five points will shape the way we talk about the content in the chapters that follow:[8]

1. *Always keep the big picture in mind.* The Bible is about a gracious God, who is sacrificially providing a way for rebels like us to dwell in his presence. There

are many other fascinating things in the Bible, but every word on every page is pointing to what God is doing through Christ. Never lose sight of the theme of God's plan of redemption through Christ as you organize your thoughts about God.

2. *Interpret the less-clear parts in light of the more-clear parts.* Survey all that Scripture says about a particular doctrine you study. That's a lot of work, but it's part of allowing the Bible to form our views about God. Along the way, you'll find passages you won't know what to do with. That's normal. Always retreat to what's clear and work your way out from there. Don't let something unclear keep you from progress. Sometimes it's OK to even set a difficult passage aside for a time. You can return to it later after praying for discernment and seeking counsel from those you respect.

3. *Mind the boundaries.* Where there is mystery, let Scripture speak for itself without trying to force a resolution that doesn't fit. Be mindful of the boundaries in Scripture so you're not always tripping over them. Let them serve as guideposts instead of trip wires. They are like a frame around a beautiful painting, intended to keep your eyes focused on what matters most. Throughout this book we will talk about these boundaries as the banks on either side of the river of orthodoxy.

4. *Don't travel alone.* When it comes to organizing our thoughts about God, we'll always need help. We stand on the shoulders of spiritual heroes, women and men of faith, who have thought deeply about the very questions we're asking. Don't neglect the resources of faithful thinkers, dead or alive, who can keep you from forming sketchy views of God.

5. *Enjoy the ride.* The study of God is intended to bring
   joy. The goal of orthodoxy is praise. Don't just study
   to learn facts but to know God better and serve him
   more faithfully. Prayerfully study God's Word so you
   can apply it, so that you might be both a hearer and
   a doer of the Word (James 1:22–25).

Orthodoxy provides guardrails around the glorious
beauty of the Christian faith. The banks of the stream help
us see the boundaries of the mystery. The waters of orthodoxy flow in a particular direction, from the source of
Scripture to our lived-out experience in the world. On your
own, you can investigate detours down the distributaries,
but in this book we will aim to flow with the current.

Between the Banks

Since we're talking about orthodoxy like a stream, I'll continue this metaphor throughout the book by also talking
about the banks on each side of the water. The shores on
either side provide boundaries for how we think about
issues that might seem difficult or even impossible for us
to fully understand. While there are a lot of things we will
have to accept as a mystery too great for words, there are
contours to these unfathomable truths.

These boundaries frame how we should talk about God.
Based on what he's revealed to us, these riverbanks mark
out what we can and can't say about God. In each section
I will discuss what I think best frames how we think about
orthodoxy related to God's word, God, and God's world.

Sometimes theologians will use the word *paradox* to
describe the tension between certain truths in the Bible. A
paradox results when two truths are difficult to make sense
of when placed side by side. One example in Scripture is that

God is in control of everything, yet humans make real decisions for which they are responsible. When you put these truths side by side, they seem to conflict with one another. That tension is what I mean when I use the word *paradox*.

I think a lot of sketchy views of God are the result of being uncomfortable with this kind of tension. Paradox can be an awkward thing to live with. We want to understand everything completely. Some seek a solution by simply ignoring the conflict. Others try to force a resolution. Throughout this book, I'm going to encourage you to embrace paradox.

When we encounter truths that seem difficult to reconcile, think of them as the banks on either side of the stream of orthodoxy. Quite often these gigantic truths set the boundaries for the mystery of God. For example, one of the biggest paradoxes is that God is three in one. Can you fit that into that cranium of yours?

With the Trinity example, one bank represents that there is only one God, and the other bank that God exists as three persons. Can our finite minds fully fathom that mystery? No. But the stream of orthodoxy flows between those boundaries. Don't ignore it or try to force a resolution. Behold its beauty!

When I was a kid my parents would take our family hiking every fall on trails high above the banks of the Missouri River in Southern Illinois. We could look across the autumn landscape to where the mighty currents of the Missouri, Illinois, and Mississippi Rivers all converged. From a high vantage point, we could see the water snaking its way between Illinois and Missouri. I hope to give you a similar perspective when it comes to thinking about God, his word, and his world.

I invite you to look to the mouth of the river, the very source of our theology, God himself, as revealed in Scripture.

Behold the Creator who made everything and needs nothing. In light of all this, I hope you stand in awe and reflect on what it means to be alive in the world today, made in the very image of God! These beliefs are all bubbling, gurgling, and flowing forward in the stream of orthodoxy.

For full disclosure, we're going to look at a lot of stuff in addition to Scripture. I love literature, philosophy, worldview studies, and of course, C. S. Lewis. I'll mix in a good bit of all those in the coming pages. I hope to illustrate what it looks like to wrestle with big ideas, while constantly coming back to the Bible as the lens through which we see everything else.

Questions to Consider

1. What direction are you facing when it comes to forming your theology?
2. What have you learned or been reminded of in this chapter that can help you better organize your thoughts about God?
3. What big truths in the Bible are essential for Christian faith?
4. What are some truths or doctrines about which Christians have liberty to disagree?
5. What are some ways you can be loving when you talk about your beliefs about God?

SECTION 1

God's Word

Chasing Elephants

*Most people catch their presuppositions
from their family and surrounding society,
the way that a child catches the measles.
But people with understanding realize that their
presuppositions should be chosen after a
careful consideration of which worldview is true.*

—FRANCIS SCHAEFFER

Did you know that you have an elephant? So do I. So does everybody. It plays a major role in how we think about everything. Put a pin in that thought for now. We will come back to it in a minute. First, let's consider how the Bible talks about itself.

In the Old Testament, the prophets often began their messages by claiming the authority that "the word of the LORD" came to them (Jeremiah 1:4; Ezekiel 1:3; Zechariah 4:8). The New Testament authors viewed the Old Testament as carrying so much authority that whether a particular noun, such as "seed," was singular or plural was extremely important (Galatians 3:16). Furthermore, the New Testament authors often put their writings on the same plain as the Old Testament (Ephesians 2:20; 2 Peter 3:15–16).

24

In other words, the biblical authors saw Scripture as the very authority of God, as if God himself were speaking through the inspired words flowing from their pens. This is really at the heart of what Christians mean when they say the Bible is inspired. You might be thinking, *all this sounds well and good, but isn't this circular reasoning?*

Circular reasoning occurs when you assume the authority of something in order to prove its authority. It's generally looked down upon as a way of arguing for the truth. Here's an example: "I believe in God because the Bible says so, and I believe the Bible because it's from God." The more someone presses back on this belief, the more you end up saying the same thing.

This form of explanation is reasoning in a circle. It's like your arguments are on autopilot in a cul-de-sac. They just keep going round and round. Your belief in God is based on your belief in the Bible, and your belief in the Bible is based on your belief in God. Can you separate the two beliefs? Should you?

Is this the kind of loop we Christians are stuck in? If the answer is yes, then are Christians unique? Are we the only people whose faith leads us to see the world in this circular way?

The answer is no. We're all guilty of circular reasoning. That's because everyone has an elephant. You have one whether you know it or not. Your secular friends have one too. And our elephants are what set the agenda for what we consider to be truth and how we make sense of life. So instead of ignoring it, let's talk about it.

The Elephant in the Room

The late Christian philosopher James Sire described this reality with a story about a boy whose mental world was disrupted when his teacher explained that the earth was not sitting on top of anything.[1] "Not sitting on anything!" The boy couldn't imagine it. Everything in his lived-out experience involved gravity. Stuff sits on top of other stuff. That's how the world works.

The boy's father wanted to have a little fun with his son. So he did what most parents do. He lied to him. Don't act so surprised. Your parents probably told you about Santa Claus or the Easter Bunny. Did you fall for the Tooth Fairy? Really?

The dad told him the earth is sitting on the back of a turtle, which is how it gets around the sun (ignore the fact that the sun isn't sitting on anything). "That's awesome!" the boy exclaimed, leaving the room in a hurry. A few minutes later he came back. "What's the turtle on, Dad?" he asked. The father then explained how the turtle is on the back of a giraffe. The boy was satisfied for a minute but then burst back in the room demanding more answers. "What's the giraffe on?" The father told him how giraffes like to ride on the back of elephants. The child left the room, only to turn around and immediately ask, "What's the elephant sitting on?" The father, knowing the gig was up, offered the only thing that might suffice. "It's just the elephant all the way down."

As you likely noticed, he didn't answer the boy's question. This story illustrates how we see the world. All worldviews begin with a certain assumption or faith commitment. If you ask enough questions, you'll eventually hit the foundation of a person's beliefs. Think of it like intellectual digging. If you're easily satisfied with superficial answers, you may never realize that every person, from a Christian to an atheist, builds their life on certain faith commitments.

Consider the words of the atheistic philosopher Crispin Sartwell who admits as much: "I have taken a leap of atheist faith," he writes.[2] What? An atheist who believes? Why would he say that? Because he knows he can't prove the basics of his atheistic view of the world. Consider the famous and dogmatic words of another skeptic, Carl Sagan, who famously said, "The Cosmos is all that is or ever was or ever will be."

These statements are all faith commitments. You can't prove any of them through science. You can't prove that there was nothing before our world came into being. You can't prove that nothing exists outside our material universe. Science can't show us that the universe is all there will ever be. Even secularists debate these three points. They are statements of faith.

These commitments are also called "presuppositions," like in the quote at the beginning of the chapter. A presupposition is something you suppose to be true before being convinced by evidence. It's a commitment that becomes authoritative to all your other views, like in the word *pre-eminent*. A presupposition is both something you believe without proof and something that holds influence over the way you understand everything else.

Presuppositions are both prior to your experience and authoritative over your experience. Everyone has presuppositions. Or, to put it differently, everyone has an elephant. Most people don't realize it. Many won't admit it. But everyone has some faith commitment, their explanation of the world that sounds a lot like, "It's just the elephant all the way down."

Are We Living in the Matrix?

So how far does this whole elephant thing go? Aren't there some things we can know with absolute certainty? Do we really have to begin with faith? Can't we begin with evidence? Can't we start with what we can see, touch, and smell?

These are all good questions, and you might be surprised, if not a little discouraged, by the answers. There's a ton of stuff we can't really prove, that we believe before being convinced by evidence.

Can you prove the world is real? Is everything around you, the chair you're sitting on, this book you're reading, the building you're in, really there? Can you prove it? Can you give evidence to make your case beyond a reasonable doubt?

I believe it's all real, but I admit I can't prove it. It could all be a figment of my imagination. It could just be inside my head. That's kind of scary, isn't it?

Have you ever had a vivid dream that seemed so real you were relieved to wake up and leave it behind? Maybe you're in that kind of dream right now? Can you prove that's not the case? You've had convincing dreams before. How can you know this isn't one of them.

Here's another one. You might be a disembodied brain in a jar. An evil scientist may have wired your brain into his supercomputer.

Everything you "experience" could simply be his dastardly designs. He's typing away right now. "You're reading a book. . . ." he types. Every argument or experiment you might give could just be that cranky scientist fiddling with your mind. Maybe this is him right now! Maybe I'm the mad scientist entering the words into your head as I'm writing them down. How would you prove that's not what's happening this very moment?

Maybe we're all in the same delusional experience together. Maybe we're living in the *Matrix*. Everything we see and touch and feel could be some alternate reality. What if we are living in some sort of virtual simulation? The billionaire entrepreneur Elon Musk believes we are living in a simulated reality. He believes the world we see and experience is a virtual simulation. Can you prove he's wrong?

You may have never considered how elephants and evil scientists illustrate the way faith plays a crucial role in how we think about the world. You probably assume this world is real. You presuppose it even. You believe it. You live as though it's real. How naïve! Just kidding. Or am I?

There's so much we can't prove. There's so much that we really can't know on our own. There are so many elephants. And everyone's elephant is the starting point for how they think about the world.

The Spectacle of Christianity

The theologian N. T. Wright uses glasses as a metaphor to describe this reality. When you wear corrective eyeglasses or sunglasses, you know they affect how you see everything. Yet, even though they change our vision of the world, we rarely think about our glasses. We just look *through* them. We never take them off and look *at* them.

That's why some of what I've discussed in this chapter might sound strange. When was the last time you thought, *I can't prove things I take for granted every day*? Instead, we

look at the world and we interpret it in light of our commitments, those things we think or wish were true. Trying to
examine your glasses might give you a headache, but I want
you to know it's not hopeless.

Everybody's got an elephant. But what if all elephants
aren't created equal? What if some faith commitments can
make sense of the world while others can't? What if some
other elephants, or presuppositions, are forever incapable
of explaining the human experience?

C. S. Lewis once said, "I believe in Christianity as
I believe that the sun has risen, not only because I see it,
but because by it I see everything else."[3] Lewis was describing how the Christian way of seeing the world, the biblical worldview, helped make sense of things for him. Lewis
became an atheist as a teenager, but as a young man he
found his atheism failed to explain the human condition—
what it feels like to be alive in the world. Once he started
with a belief in God as a basic belief, instead of starting with
atheism, things came into focus.

In contrast, consider the ideas of an atheistic professor
from Duke University. Dr. Alex Rosenberg wrote a book to
explain why he's an atheist and what difference it's made in
his view of the world. It's called *The Atheist's Guide to Reality: Enjoying Life without Illusions.* Dr. Rosenberg believes
that only the physical world is real and that everything that
can't be proven by science must be a delusion.

That shouldn't affect too much, should it? You can probably tell I'm being a little cheeky. Rosenberg's belief affects
everything. Where you start, what elephant you choose to
base your beliefs on, sets the framework for how you make
sense of everything.

Rosenberg says science can't explain the idea that we are
persons, that we make real decisions, that truth and meaning are real, or that moral distinctions exist. So, since we

should only believe in things science can explain, we should reject personhood, free will, meaning, and morality as delusions. That covers all that matters most in life, doesn't it?

Consider this scenario: You see a young boy help an elderly person with a cane to get across the street. That looks like a good deed, right? Then imagine the boy takes the elderly person's cane and beats them to the ground with it and steals their money. That's a bad deed, right? How does this whole account look from behind Rosenberg's worldview glasses?

Since the boy doesn't have personhood, you can't really blame him. Since he can't make real decisions, there's no guilt or blame. Since there's no meaning in the world, there's no moral to the story. And since there are no moral distinctions, we shouldn't say one act was better than the other. Rosenberg would have us believe it's all just a bunch of delusional thinking.

For C. S. Lewis, reducing everything to scientific explanations could never account for the richness of life. This is sometimes referred to as *scientific reductionism*. As a young man, C. S. Lewis grew dissatisfied with his atheistic view of the world for these very reasons. While science can be a helpful way to think about certain physical realities, like the law of gravity, it can't make sense of everything.

Science can't even make sense of what matters most. No one gets out of bed and lives for the law of gravity, although without gravity you'd be peeling yourself off the ceiling each morning. No one hits the day with gusto because of the temperature at which water boils. That's important if you want a cup of tea. Other than that, you probably don't think about it much.

So, what do you get out of bed for? Of course, school, work, and parents can all be motivating factors. But you probably spend much of your day motivated by friendships,

responsibilities, purpose, calling, duty, and delight. Rosenberg would say such things aren't real. They're just illusions that help us survive—happy accidents, whatever that
means.

C. S. Lewis left his atheistic assumptions, his godless
elephant, behind in search of a way to see the world that
could make sense of it and his place in it. He found it in
Christianity, a worldview that made sense of the human
experience.

This basic instinct to see the world outside of us as actually being there and being real is not a delusion. It really
is there. And as the apostle John tells us, it's a world God
loves very much (John 3:16). But the Bible also tells us that
it's a world created good but that has gone bad. It's a world
filled with moral distinctions of good and evil. This Christian way of seeing the world fit hand in glove for C. S. Lewis
in making sense of both the beauty and the horrors of life.

The Christian Elephant

If everyone has an elephant, what does a Christian elephant
look like? What assumptions do believers make in the way
they see the world? Just like atheists have certain fundamental commitments that prop up their beliefs, Christians do
too. Here's a concise description of basic Christian beliefs:
God exists, he's personal, and he's revealed himself in a way
we can know him personally.

If any of these commitments are wrong, then Christianity can't be true. To put it another way, you can't be described
as a Christian if you don't believe these basic truths. If you
don't believe God exists, you're better described as an atheist. If you believe God exists but is not personal, then you're
a deist. But if you believe God exists and is personal, then
the notion of revelation, or Scripture, isn't far-fetched at all.

If God exists and is personal, then revelation flows naturally from your beliefs. This is the sort of God who would reveal himself.

To be a Christian is to operate within these three faith commitments. Yet I believe the Christian can have far more certainty than simply taking a blind leap of faith. Here's how: if the Bible is true, then its claim that Christians have the Holy Spirit within them is also true (John 14:15–17). The Bible teaches that the Spirit gives believers certainty about the truth of the gospel (Romans 8:16).

Some of you may know what I'm talking about. This is the kind of claim that surely sounds incredible to a skeptic. It will continue to sound absurd unless they experience it themselves. Then and only then will they have certainty it's true.

That's why when I have the opportunity to share the gospel with someone who doesn't believe in God, I'll encourage them to consider reading through the Gospel of John and praying a prayer like, "God, if you exist, please help me understand what I read." I tell them the prayer isn't magical. It will neither turn them into a newt nor a Christian. And if God doesn't exist, then what do they have to fear? But if God does exist, and if the Bible is more than just a book, and if God does work in the world through his Spirit, then who knows what might happen?

If a personal God exists who has revealed himself in a way we can know him, then this revelation must be powerful. Of course, the Bible makes this very claim for itself. "The Word of God is living and effective," the writer of Hebrews tells us, "and sharper than any double-edged sword, penetrating as far as the separation of soul and spirit, joints and marrow. It is able to judge the thoughts and intentions of the heart" (Hebrews 4:12).

Some of you are clever enough to see this is a circular argument. It is, and I don't even feel bad about it. I won't lose any sleep over it. In fact, I sleep better knowing it's true.

This is the Christian elephant. And it's this elephant all the way down. God has revealed himself in such a way that we can have certainty in our knowledge of who he is. In light of that, we can begin to understand who we are. That's the key to unlocking reality.

For the Christian, the starting point is a personal God who has made himself known. Our beliefs about God are fundamental to what we believe about everything else. That's not to say there aren't supporting reasons for why you believe the Bible as a Christian. We will get to those in time. For now, you need to know this Christian way of seeing things doesn't require you to deny the human experience—within you or around you. It makes sense of it and dignifies it.

Theology's Handmaiden

Not only do I love theology, but I also appreciate philosophy. An old expression from the Middle Ages aptly summarizes my view of the two: "Theology is the queen of the sciences, and philosophy is her handmaiden."[4] "Queen of the sciences" means theology is the supreme way we know things about the world. We begin with God and the Bible, but we don't have to end there. We can learn things from other sources like science, while recognizing that God has revealed true things about himself, establishing the authority for how we make sense of everything else.

As you might imagine, those who don't believe in God aren't fond of theology being placed on top. In his book *Beyond Good and Evil*, the atheistic philosopher Friedrich

Nietzsche predicted psychology would become the main way people made sense of the world. He said it would become the "queen of the sciences."[5] Sadly, for the most part, Nietzsche was right. A lot of people trust their inner thoughts and feelings as the ultimate way to make sense of things.

In a lot of ways, this book illustrates how this idea creeps into the church and how some Christians frame their thoughts about God. We want to avoid doing theology "Nietzsche style," where we let our own inner thoughts be the chief authority for how we understand God, the world, and our place in it. If God exists and has revealed himself, then theology should indeed be the ultimate way we make sense of it all.

What we believe about God from the Bible should be our elephant, our main authority. But there are situations in life that aren't clearly addressed in the Bible. For example, the Bible doesn't give immediate directions on things like artificial intelligence or animal cloning. That's where philosophy can be useful.

Philosophy simply means the love of wisdom. Philosophy is all about asking important questions. When I teach an introduction to philosophy course to college students, I give my first lecture at a cemetery. I ask students why philosophy matters and let them think for a few minutes before giving an answer.

"Philosophy matters because it addresses the most important questions in life, which all have expiration dates," I would say. Then I would point to the headstones surrounding us and say, "that was her expiration date," and then "that was his expiration date." We all have a limited amount of time to figure out life. Our unanswered questions die with us.

If philosophy is about asking questions, theology is primarily concerned with providing answers. That's how philosophy is like a handmaiden to theology. Philosophy often functions like a question mark. Theology works more like a period or even at times like an exclamation point. The two pair nicely in helping us explore how we think and consider where we can find answers. But it's important to get them in the right order.

Philosophy's Funnel

There are three big categories we can divide philosophy into: metaphysics, epistemology, and axiology. I know, those three words can be a mouthful. **Metaphysics** is the biggest of all topics about what is really real. "Meta" means the comprehensive or total reality or truth. If you believe there is a God, then that is where your metaphysics begins. If you believe there is no God and all that really exists is the material universe, that is your metaphysic.

When you think metaphysics, think elephant. This is sometimes referred to as "ultimate reality." If God exists, as I of course believe he does, then he is clearly the ultimate reality. If the universe is all that exists, then it is the ultimate reality. But whatever you begin with, whether as an atheist or a Christian, your belief about what's most important sets the boundaries for all that follows.

Epistemology is the branch of philosophy that deals with *how* we know what we know. It's based on the root word that means knowledge. **Axiology** is the area of philosophy that deals with what we believe is beautiful in terms of both art and human actions. These three branches of philosophy work kind of like a funnel. What you believe about reality (*metaphysics*) guides how you know things (*epistemology*) and sets the boundaries for all the beliefs that follow (including *axiology*).

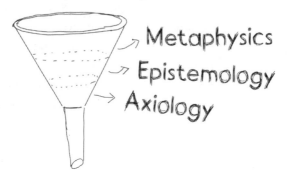

Metaphysics
Epistemology
Axiology

If your metaphysic begins with God, then you will believe that you know things because God has revealed the information. If, on the other hand, you begin with the commitment that God doesn't exist (for instance, if your metaphysic is deistic or atheistic), your epistemology (your way to know true things) will mostly focus on what you can learn through the study of the world in science.

Here are two examples of great thinkers whose rejection of the possibility of God affects their view of knowledge. The prolific philosopher Bertrand Russell once said, "What science cannot discover, mankind cannot know."[6] Alex Rosenberg, the professor of philosophy I mentioned earlier, said something similar, "Physics fixes all the facts."[7]

Both statements sound really sophisticated. If the world is all that exists, we can only learn things about it through science or physics. If we can't prove something through science, then it can't be a fact. The physical sciences determine what should be considered real. You can see how their view of metaphysics sets the boundaries for their epistemology.

But wait a minute. Did Russell and Rosenberg learn these guiding values through science? No. These are beliefs that aren't themselves based on science. They are philosophical commitments—beliefs they bring to their study of the world—beliefs that can't be proven by science, faith commitments that reveal their elephant.

Furthermore, their views can't live up to their own standards. Let me outline it this way: (1) Neither statement by Russell or Rosenberg can be proven by science or physics. And, (2) according to them, if you can't prove something by science or physics, then it isn't something you can know; it isn't a fact. Therefore, (3) since you can't prove their statements by science or physics, then they are really just admitting they have an elephant. But we already knew that, didn't we?

Russell and Rosenberg believe the physical world is all there is. There is no God. There is nothing but a natural world. That's why they reduce everything down to what can be learned or proven through science. But don't be fooled. They didn't discover their guiding value, that science is the only way to know things, through a microscope or a telescope. It's a faith commitment (*metaphysics*) that determines how they see the world (*epistemology*). And it drives what they think is good and beautiful (*axiology*).

For the Christian, we believe God has shown us what is good and what the Lord requires of us (Micah 6:8). As Christians we begin with God (*metaphysics*). We can know true things about the world because God has made us and the world in such a way that we can seek after truth (*epistemology*). Because God is personal, he has revealed true things that frame the way we think about the world and how we should live in it (*axiology*). In this way, Christianity provides a total philosophy for life.

If this world is not all there is, then how we live and know things should not just be based on what we can see in front of us. But how can we know what all that means? The British theologian J. S. Whale summed it up really well when he said, "But *who* God is, God himself must tell us in revelation or we shall never know . . . . Christian doctrine agrees that there is no experience of God without a revelation from God."[8] If we, as created beings, are to know anything about reality, what is good or beautiful, or how to live, we need our Creator to reveal it to us. We desperately need God to make himself known.

A Study in Contrasts: God's World and God's Word

Christians believe just this—that God has made himself known. But how exactly has he done this? Let's look to C. S. Lewis's favorite psalm. He described Psalm 19 as the greatest of all the Psalms and one of the best poems in all the world.[9] We're going to survey this Psalm to illustrate the very point I've been trying to make.

This psalm contrasts what God has revealed about himself in nature and what he has revealed about himself in Scripture. I think you'll plainly see where the emphasis lies between the two. Let's begin by looking at verses 1–6:

> The heavens declare the glory of God,
> and the expanse proclaims the work of his hands.
> Day after day they pour out speech;
> night after night they communicate knowledge.
> There is no speech; there are no words;
> their voice is not heard.

Their message has gone out to the whole earth,
and their words to the ends of the world.
In the heavens he has pitched a tent for the sun.
It is like a bridegroom coming from his home;
it rejoices like an athlete running a course.
It rises from one end of the heavens
and circles to their other end;
nothing is hidden from its heat. (Psalm 19:1–6)

Seeing Nature

When David looks at the world God made, he senses the very glory of God. He sees God's message spreading over the whole world in the rising and setting of the sun. He goes so far as to say nature is communicating knowledge (19:2). But just how much knowledge about God can we learn from the rising and setting sun?

This is a point a lot of people skip over. David says the messengers of God in nature, things like the sun and sky, have no speech or words (19:3). He says their voice is not heard. Nature is pointing us beyond itself, but we can't understand its message. When we watch a beautiful sunset, we might get a sense of God's power, but we can't learn anything new about his character or work in the world.

Learning Scripture

David does something very interesting in the following verses. He moves from nature to Scripture. The contrast is clear. While the message of nature, what theologians call "general revelation" is limited, the message of Scripture, what theologians call "special revelation," is described as perfect. Look at verses 7–9:

The instruction of the LORD is perfect,
renewing one's life;
the testimony of the LORD is trustworthy,
making the inexperienced wise.
The precepts of the LORD are right,
making the heart glad;
the command of the LORD is radiant,
making the eyes light up.
The fear of the LORD is pure,
enduring forever;
the ordinances of the LORD are reliable
and altogether righteous.
They are more desirable than gold—
than an abundance of pure gold;
and sweeter than honey
dripping from a honeycomb. (Psalm 19:7-10)

What a comparison! While the voice of nature has no words, the Word of God is described as perfect and trustworthy in verse seven, right and radiant in verse eight, and pure and everlasting in verse nine. Just look at what God's Word accomplishes here. It renews our life and makes the inexperienced wise. It makes the heart glad and enlightens our spiritual eyes. There's really no contest between nature and Scripture. Yet the two are not in conflict. They sing in harmony.

David isn't yet finished with comparing God's world and God's Word. In seeking to describe how great Scripture is, he surveys the most valuable commodities on earth. God's Word is more valuable than gold and sweeter than honey (19:10). Which is more beneficial to the believer—nature or Scripture? This passage makes it clear how David would answer:

Who perceives his unintentional sins?
Cleanse me from my hidden faults.
Moreover, keep your servant from willful sins;
do not let them rule me.
Then I will be blameless
and cleansed from blatant rebellion.
May the words of my mouth
and the meditation of my heart
be acceptable to you,
LORD, my rock and my Redeemer. (Psalm 19:12–14)

Knowing God

Even in the close of this holy poem in Psalm 19, we find the contrast continued. David calls God his rock. That's a pretty simple term to understand. God is our foundation and our stability, like standing on a sturdy boulder. This is an example from nature to picture the stability we have in God.

Then David calls God his Redeemer. To understand that term, we really need the whole biblical story to show how God promised to forgive his people of their sins and rescue them from bondage. This second reference is spiritual. Here again we see nature and Scripture working together in harmony.

There's something else you should see here before we move on, which ties in with the theme we began with in this section about how God reveals himself to us. When David calls God "LORD" in the final verse, it's written in all caps. Why is that? I'm glad you asked. It's because the word in the original Hebrew language is "Yahweh." That's the name God revealed to Moses when he spoke to him through a burning bush. Without revelation we can't know God personally.

In Romans 1 Paul tells us God made the world to reveal something about himself, namely, his power and his divine nature. But he further explains that no one is seeking God in nature and that all of us have fallen short of God's standard. We might read Romans and throw our hands up in despair and ask, "How can we ever know God in a personal way?"

Paul answers this question in Romans 10:17, "So faith comes from what is heard, and what is heard comes through the message about Christ." The way to know God personally is not by merely looking at the sunrise in the morning or the stars at night, or even at a bush ignited by God himself. We need to hear God's voice. His voice, Christians believe, is recorded for us in the Bible.

Nature is saying something about God, but because we are sinners and live in a fallen world, we are never going to interpret its message correctly. We need God to speak clearly to us. That's why our theology, the way we organize our thoughts about God, begins with Scripture, God's revelation of himself. But why do we believe the Bible is inspired by God?

Why Do You Believe the Bible?

As I said earlier, we all have an elephant. For the Christian, our elephant is a personal God who has revealed himself. Instead of studying the world from our limited human perspective and trying to reason upward and outward to the rest of the universe, we believe there's such a thing as top-down information. If God exists, then he's able to communicate to us from outside the system, from outside of nature.

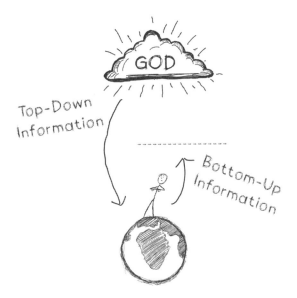

It's really important that we think about why we believe what we do. Though everyone has an elephant, the Christian should be prepared to give a well-reasoned answer when someone asks why we believe in the God of the Bible. That's why I've devoted a few chapters in this book to helping you think about the Bible—what it is and how it came to be.

When I'm asked why I believe the Bible, I like to lead with my top five and start by just being honest:

1. **I believe the Bible because I'm a Christian.** As we've discussed, it's my elephant. Everyone has one. My belief in God, Jesus, and the Bible are all connected. I like to admit up front that I have a certain assumption about how I see the world. I believe God exists, is personal, and has revealed himself in nature, history, and Scripture. These are the glasses that color the way I see the world. That's my presupposition.

2. **I believe the Bible because I've seen its power.** I've seen the Bible radically transform people's lives. God uses his revelation of himself to change people's lives. I've seen God use the Bible to turn a tenured literature professor at a prestigious university from an atheist to a pastor's wife. And I've experienced this power myself. Becoming a Christian and reading the Bible has changed the way I see the world, the people in it, and how I think about my life under God's authority. Time is too short and space is too limited to show you the countless examples of the Bible's power in people's lives. If you're a Christian, I'm sure you can think of several yourself.

3. **The third reason I believe the Bible is because it makes sense out of life.** I like to call this "the explanatory power of the Christian home." As C. S. Lewis explained, it's like the sun that shines light on everything else. Seeing the world through the lens of the Bible has a way of making sense of things. So, yes, it's a presupposition or an elephant, but it provides us with a key to making sense of the human experience, whereas other assumptions about reality do not. Can the same be said of other ways of seeing the world? If there is no God, then it's difficult, if not impossible, to make sense of the human experience and our longing for purpose and meaning. But if there is a God, if he has revealed himself, then the human condition isn't an illusion. Instead of seeing human values like dignity and equality as meaningless, these things make sense because God created us in his image and endowed us with intrinsic worth.

4. **The fourth reason I believe the Bible is because a lot of evidence proves its accuracy and reliability.** This is the point some of you have been waiting for. I don't

start here because having more evidence is not why I personally started believing. But it can be helpful. And there's plenty of it to be found. For example, there's more evidence for the Bible being reliably copied and transmitted through the centuries than there is for any other ancient writing. If we doubt that the Bible is a reliable document accurately recording what the disciples believed, then we'd have to reject all the major works of literature from ancient Greek philosophy to poetry. There is good reason to trust the Bible based on evidence. I'll say more about that in the next chapter.

5. **Finally, I believe the Bible because Jesus rose from the dead**. It must have been breathtaking for Jesus's disciples to see him after the resurrection. Even though Jesus reveals to them several times that he would rise on the third day, they certainly appear surprised when he shows up. How did these disciples make sense of Jesus's resurrection? They looked to the Scriptures. They didn't say, "Well, we have Jesus now risen from the dead; who needs the Scriptures?" No, their belief in the Bible, in this case, the Old Testament, was foundational to how they thought about Jesus's resurrection.

Consider our oldest creed, a summary of Christian belief, in the history of the Christian church. This is the creed Paul receives shortly after he first becomes a Christian (Acts 9). As a new follower of Jesus, Paul is mentored by other disciples who lived in Jerusalem. He later wrote about what they taught him in his first letter to the Corinthians:

For I passed on to you as most important what I also received: that Christ died for our sins according to the Scriptures, that he was buried, and that he was raised on the third day according to the Scriptures. (1 Corinthians 15:3–4, CSB)

Even atheist historians admit this creed had to have been developed within a few years of the resurrection at the latest.[10] Its historical origin in the early days after the resurrection is accepted among both Christian and non-Christian scholars. Belief that Jesus rose from the dead is not an idea the disciples came up with decades later, but something they believed very early on. It's a belief that can be traced back to the first Easter.

Don't miss the emphasis in the creed from 1 Corinthians. The disciples aren't saying, "Hey, just believe Jesus rose from the dead. Don't worry about the Scriptures." No! These early disciples believed Jesus died for their sins—*according to the Scriptures*.

People die every day. Why was Jesus's death so important? It was important for them because they saw it as the fulfillment of the Old Testament prophecies. The disciples viewed the life, death, and resurrection of Jesus through the lens of the Old Testament Scriptures. That was their elephant. The resurrection mattered greatly because of how it was made sense of *according to the Old Testament Scriptures*.

Jesus loved the Old Testament Scriptures too. I've heard it said that Jesus quoted from every book in the Old Testament either in word or principle. I don't doubt that, though I've never tried to validate this claim. Not only did Jesus love the Old Testament, he's also the one who commissioned everything you see throughout the rest of the New Testament (Matthew 28:19–20). He commanded his disciples to go into the whole world teaching everything he taught, and then promised the Spirit would remind them of all they learned and lead them into all truth (John 14:26).

If Jesus rose from the dead, as the first disciples believed and as Scripture explains, then we should love the book Jesus loved (the Old Testament) and the book Jesus commissioned (the New Testament). We aren't above the first disciples and their commitment to Scripture. And we certainly aren't above Jesus. So the best thing we can do is to place ourselves beneath the authority of the Bible and allow it to challenge us and to build us up in the way that only it can do.

If God exists, as I believe he does, and if he has revealed himself, as I believe he has, then Scripture should be our main source for organizing our thoughts about God.

Final Tension

In this chapter, we've thought about how we as humans can start to make sense of the world and the human experience by beginning with God's Word. It's the Christian elephant. While the heavens reveal the glory of God (Psalm 19), the sun and sky aren't saying much. We need God to reveal himself in words we can understand. That's what we believe God has done in the Bible. But how can we make sense of the Bible?

The Bible is a divine book, but it's also a human book. God is the ultimate author of the Bible, yet he used humans to write and organize his words in the way we have them today. It's really impossible to separate these categories. And we shouldn't want to. As the theologian Norman Geisler warns, we should avoid "denying or diminishing [the Bible's] divine characteristics while affirming its human traits, or else affirming its divine properties while denying or diminishing its human traits."[11]

When it comes to the Bible, the two banks on either side of the stream of orthodoxy are its divine author, God, and then its human authors like Paul and Moses. In the next chapter, we'll focus on the divine side of Scripture. Then, in the following chapter, we'll look more at the human side of the Bible. God's Word is a product of both.

Questions to Consider

1. What is an elephant (not the kind with a trunk and tusks, but the kind described in this chapter)?
2. How does Psalm 19 show the necessity of God's Word, even as it celebrates what can be learned about God from creation?
3. In what ways is Christianity superior to atheism in explaining the human experience?
4. In what ways are theology and philosophy similar and different in making sense of the world?
5. Why do you believe the Bible?

Three Divine Eyes

Do not defend God's word, but testify to it. Trust the Word.
It is a ship loaded to the very limits of its capacity.
—DIETRICH BONHOEFFER

After I graduated from seminary, I landed my first full-time job as a student pastor at a church in Nashville, Tennessee. We lived in the house of Hank Williams, Sr., a famous country music star. It was a big house, and it's a long story. More about that later.

One day, I took students from my church to a youth camp. The speaker walked on stage, held up his Bible, and said, "This is God's inspired, inerrant, and infallible Word." I remember seeing a sea of glazed looks on the students' faces and thinking, "No one here knows what this guy means by those 'I' words." I wasn't even sure if the speaker, if asked, could define them himself.

Why do people use such complicated words to describe the Bible? For example, scholars use the term *perspicuity* when referring to the simplicity of the Bible. That sure makes sense, doesn't it? The youth speaker should have added the word *perspicuity* to his list!

But if you know what these three "I" words mean, you can better understand the divine side of the Bible. I'm going to make a case that these terms reflect the way the Bible talks about itself. After all, what we believe about the Bible should line up with what the Bible says about itself.

The Perfect Fit

Think about how important the Bible is for a Christian— how important it might be for you. As a believer, you're probably doing your best to practice the principles you've found in the Bible. Surely this is an aim you'll carry into your future career. If you get married, you'll probably want to be with someone who will share these same values. On top of all that, you are basing your beliefs about where you'll spend eternity on the Bible. That's a whole lot to put on one book, isn't it?

The Bible was written thousands of years ago, in languages you can't read, in places you will likely never visit. And you trust it? You trust it for how you live your life, conduct yourself in a career, raise a family, and your very eternity? If you're a Christian, you place a whole lot of faith in that ancient book. I do too.

As I shared in the last chapter, there are several reasons I trust the Bible. To borrow an old expression, I'm putting all my eggs in that basket. Or to put it better, the apostle Paul says, "Let God be true, and every man a liar" (Romans 3:4, NIV 1984). That's a helpful way to think about it, isn't it? We trust God even if others think we're crazy.

I sometimes hear Christian parents fret about their children's beliefs. While I understand their concern, I think we can unwittingly treat the Bible like it's a fragile heirloom, as though it should be protected in bubble wrap and hidden in the attic for some future time when it's taken out and given to the next generation. The Bible isn't fragile. It's survived for centuries, even where cultures sought to destroy it. We need it far more than it needs us.

Inspiration

If the Bible were going to defend itself, what might it say? For starters, it claims to be from God. Think about how the Old Testament prophets talked about their messages. Prophets like Jeremiah, Ezekiel, and Zechariah prefaced their speeches with, "The Word of the LORD came to me" (see Jeremiah 1:4; Ezekiel 12:1; Zechariah 4:8).

This signified that they weren't speaking on their own authority. Their words were from God. That's a tall claim to make, particularly when they faced capital punishment if their prophecies didn't come true (Deuteronomy 18:20). In short, if these prophets weren't really passing along God's words, it would become obvious over time, and the prophets would pay the ultimate price with their very lives.

The prophet Samuel describes his message by saying that the Spirit of the Lord spoke through him by placing the words on his tongue (2 Samuel 23:2). This is referred to as *inspiration*. It means God is the ultimate author of the Bible. Like the Old Testament prophets, the New Testament authors also claimed to be speaking on behalf of God.

The apostle Peter describes it this way: "Above all, you know this: No prophecy of Scripture comes from the prophet's own interpretation, because no prophecy ever came by the will of man; instead, men spoke from God as they were carried along by the Holy Spirit" (2 Peter 1:20–21). Peter believed the Old Testament prophets were speaking from God. But later he claims the same status for the message of the New Testament: "so that you recall the words previously spoken by the holy prophets and the command of our Lord and Savior given through your apostles" (2 Peter 3:2).

Peter places the Old Testament prophets, the words of Jesus (the Gospels), and the words of the apostles (the epistles) on the same level. In short, Peter believes God was the ultimate author of the Old and New Testaments. The apostle Paul makes the same claim when he tells Timothy, "All Scripture is inspired by God" (2 Timothy 3:16).

The prophets and the apostles saw Scripture as a book with a divine author and themselves as servants of God's message. God is the ultimate author of the Bible. That's what we mean when we say the Bible is inspired.

Now I will tell you a few things we don't believe about inspiration. We aren't talking about the kind of inspiration experienced by great thinkers like Aristotle or Shakespeare. By inspiration we don't mean creative genius. The Bible authors didn't just have sensitive intuitions. They weren't inspired in some generic way like a great artist creating a work of art. Christians believe that God breathed out his message in such a way that the prophets and apostles passed on God's own words to others. That's why Christians believe God is the ultimate author of the Bible.

Some might think inspiration means that God gave the big ideas of the Bible, but he didn't inspire the words. For example, God could inspire the biblical authors to write about redemption and forgiveness without guiding them in the words they'd use. This is similar to what I do in my class assignments. I often have students write a paper instead of taking a final exam. I give them general parameters for the paper, but I don't micromanage the words they write.

The problem with this view related to Scripture is that the only way we get access to the big ideas of the Bible is through the words. If we can't trust the words, why should we trust the big ideas? We only know about the big ideas because of all the little words that make up the Bible.

When we use the term *inspiration*, we mean God gave human authors not only the big idea of the Bible but the very words they used to describe those big ideas. So inspiration means God inspired *all* the words of the *entire* Bible. This is a view known as *verbal plenary inspiration*. Verbal means words. Plenary means all. God communicated his message to the biblical authors in such a way as to give us confidence in his message for us. So how did that work exactly?

Inerrancy

God didn't pick up Moses by the ankles, flip him upside down, dunk his head in ink, and use him like a fountain pen. The apostle John didn't fall into some hypnotic trance and start writing his gospel without ever being aware of what he was doing. That's not what we mean by inspiration. There's another "I" word that will make this clearer.

Inerrancy is a technical word that means God used the biblical authors to write exactly what he wanted them to write without error. God directed them so that the words communicated his message without error. Paul tells Timothy that "all Scripture is inspired by God" (2 Timothy 3:16). Paul doesn't make a distinction between words and big ideas. He credits God for all of it.

Autographs

So when Moses sat down to write the first five books of the Bible, God inspired all that he wrote. That's inspiration. Here's the problem. We don't have the original documents Moses wrote. That sounds like a massive problem. Don't freak out just yet. I'm about to explain why we can still trust the accuracy of our Bibles today.

The original documents written by the biblical authors are called the *autographs*. Think of it like a signature or autograph you might get from a celebrity. When the person signs their name, that's called an autograph. If you made a copy of their signature and claimed it was original, you'd be lying. That would be called a forgery.

Our claim that God used human authors to write what he wanted them to say in no way means that people who copied what they wrote wouldn't ever make a mistake. Inspiration was an event, the moment when the biblical authors wrote their original writings. Inspiration has nothing to do with people making copies of Scripture.

The belief that God inspired the biblical authors to write without error only applies to when they were originally writing the Bible. In other words, if someone picked up Paul's letter of Romans and started copying it, Christians don't believe God was inspiring them in the copying process.

For example, if you were to take a book of the Bible and make a handmade copy, you would soon discover you are not inspired. You are not inerrant. You are going to make mistakes. You'll probably make a lot of them. That's OK; you're human. But our belief about the biblical authors is not that they are more than human, but that the Bible is more than a mere human product.

My college students often use what are called *journibles*. These are journals that have a passage of Scripture on one page with blank pages to copy the passage by hand. I like to tell them that God didn't inspire their *journibles*. Their handmade copies are wonderful. But they are far from perfect. My students sometimes misspell things. Sometimes they skip a word, or even a line. Their copies can differ greatly from the passages of Scripture they are copying.

Trustworthy copies

If God inspired the autographs, this should be pretty straightforward, right? All we have to do is get our hands on those original writings and we're set. But what do we do if we don't have the autographs? You should know this isn't just a problem for the Bible but for all ancient texts.

Scholars who authenticate ancient texts look for a couple things to work their way back to the originals. They get as many copies of the ancient documents they can find, looking for those as close to the date of the original writings as possible. Before we look at the evidence for the Bible, let's consider some other popular ancient writings.

Consider Greek philosophy. Universities the world over have philosophy majors. They all study the writings of Plato. How much evidence do we have for Plato? We have a couple hundred ancient copies of Plato's writings. How old is our oldest copy? It's from about one thousand years after Plato originally wrote it.

So we have about a couple hundred copies with a thousand-year gap between the originals and our first existing copies. That's not bad for ancient documents. Universities study these writings as reliable sources for what Plato taught.

Let's consider another ancient author, the poet Homer. There is more and older evidence for Homer's epic poetry than any author outside the Bible. We have around two thousand ancient copies of Homer's writing, and it's way closer to the original than anything we have for Plato. Plus, the oldest copy only goes back about five hundred years from the original. That's pretty impressive.

So how does the Bible line up? As I've already implied, we don't have any of the originals for it either. The original letters Paul wrote? All of them gone. The original gospel accounts? Gone. What are we to do? We can do the same thing with the Bible that scholars do with the works of Plato or Homer. How does the evidence for the Bible compare?

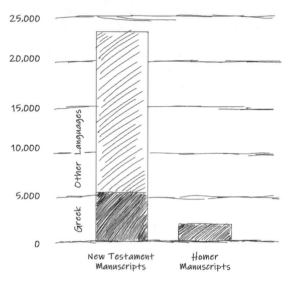

To cut to the chase, the New Testament puts the evidence for Homer and Plato to shame. We have a mountain of literary evidence—over twenty thousand ancient copies of the New Testament in the original language (Greek) and in several other languages into which it was translated at a very early stage. One book by Princeton University scholar Bruce Metzger outlines all these early copies in other languages. It's fittingly called, *The Early Versions of the New Testament*.[1]

Some skeptics will point out that all these ancient copies have issues. Just like I tell my students that God didn't inspire their *journibles*, God didn't inspire these scribes who made copies of Scripture. All the copies have differences. We might call them mistakes. Scholars call them textual variants. Most of them relate to spelling and grammar.

For example, many scribes weren't very good at spelling. Sometimes a scribe would spell one word three different ways—in a single verse! There are even places where we can tell a scribe made an intentional change for one reason or another. And the more copies you have, the more typos and mistakes you're going to find.

Now, for full disclosure, there are some places where Bible scholars have important questions about what existed in the originals. But those places are very few and far between. Most scholars agree what was originally written has been established with 99-percent accuracy. And none of the remaining questions deal with a major Christian doctrine.

If you read your Bible carefully, you'll notice that the scholars who translated the Scriptures call out the verses where there are issues in the copies. For example, there are a few verses in Mark's and John's gospels where translators point out that they can't be traced back to the oldest documents. If you read the footnotes in most modern copies of the Bible, the scholars will make this clear. No one is trying to cover it up.

If you see a Bible verse in italics or brackets, read the note at the bottom of the page, and you can get a feel for the sort of issues the Bible translators dealt with in getting back to the originals, the autographs. None of them affect a core doctrine of the Christian faith.

All these mistakes don't really add up to a major problem. Like with other ancient writings, we can get back to what was originally written by comparing the copies. And if you're wondering, yes, there are these kinds of mistakes in other ancient writings too.

If someone says we can't trust that the Bible was reliably passed down through the ages, they would have to apply the same standard to the rest of literature from the ancient world. If we can trust the writings of Plato and Homer, we have far greater reason to trust that the writings of the Bible have been accurately passed down. To put it another way, if we can't trust the Bible, we can't trust any ancient writing!

Sometimes students will protest, "But those other documents don't make such big claims on our lives." That's a good point, but it's not entirely accurate. If you read Greek philosophy, you'll see they really did care about trying to live "the good life." They thought deeply about what goodness is and how we should live our lives pursuing it. Just because the Bible makes big claims doesn't mean it should be held to a different standard than other literature.

Let's pretend we made the Bible the standard for all other literature. What if every ancient writing, to be considered trustworthy, was required to have twenty thousand ancient copies in different languages, with some manuscripts dating to within a century of the original like the New Testament does? How many would measure up? None. None of them could measure up to the quality of evidence we have for the Bible!

Inerrancy means God inspired these biblical authors to write, without error, exactly what he wanted. That's a big claim, but it's one the Bible makes for itself. And there's a massive amount of evidence, far more than for any other ancient writing, that what they wrote down has been reliably copied and passed down to us today.

Infallibility

We've pointed out the powerful things God is able to do with his message. What about the things God can't do? Have you thought about that before?

God can't make a square circle. Odd, isn't it? God can't create a married bachelor. Weird, I know. In other words, God can't do stupid stuff. He can't defy logic. That's because logic flows from the mind of God. Square circles and married bachelors are illogical. So, quite naturally, God can't do dumb stuff like creating something illogical.

The Bible talks about some stuff God can't do. For example, the apostle Paul says God cannot lie (Titus 1:2) or deny himself (2 Timothy 2:13).

God can't create a four-sided triangle. God can't make a stone too heavy for him to lift. And God can't lie. That's because God cannot deny himself. He cannot do things that are inconsistent with his character. The only limit to what God can do is God!

True truth

Here's how all this applies to the Bible. The belief that the Bible is infallible supports the conviction that Scripture reflects God's character. If God exists, and is personal, and has revealed himself to us, then his revelation reflects who he is. And if God can't lie, then his Word is incapable of lying to us. It follows then, that if God is the ultimate author of the Bible, then the Bible accurately reflects God.

You might wonder, *how can God be the ultimate author of the Bible if he used humans to write his message?* The Bible explains that God spoke to and through the biblical authors to communicate his message. That means there is a dual authorship to the Bible. It is 100 percent from God. It is 100 percent from humans.

God doesn't waste anything. He used all the biblical authors were: their life experience, their cumulative vocabulary at the time of their writing, their writing style, their setting in history, and their personalities to write exactly what God wanted them to write without error. Their humanity was not turned off while they wrote Scripture.

We have good reason to trust the Bible. That doesn't mean we always understand it or that it never challenges the assumptions of our day. But as Christians, we believe deep down that God exists, is personal, and has revealed himself. So we approach the Bible with trust in God, even when encountering those points that feel uncomfortable or confusing.

If God exists, and if he is personal, and if he has revealed himself, then we must receive the Bible as a reflection of God's very character. It's trustworthy because he is trustworthy. That doesn't mean we can always understand it, or reconcile it with every experience in the world, but we can trust it. I love how the late theologian R. C. Sproul used to talk about faith as well-reasoned trust.[2] We have good reasons to trust God's Word.

Why Doesn't God Just Speak to Me?

One time I remember asking God for something very specific. My parents had just gotten a divorce, and I was in the process of transferring colleges. I felt so alone I prayed God would send someone to my apartment, anyone really, to be an encouragement to me. No one ever came. I remember sitting all alone and feeling like a small part of my faith died that night.

Maybe you've felt a bit like that before too. Have you ever wondered why God doesn't just talk to us today, the way he talked to people in the past? Wouldn't that be better? Wouldn't you have a lot more confidence about the decisions you need to make if you could hear a voice from heaven? Certainly, if God has done it before he could do it again.

The truth is, if God did speak to you tonight, it would seem amazing in the moment. I have no doubt. But you would spend the rest of your life second-guessing your experience. You would wonder, *Did it really happen?* Not only would you second-guess it, you'd be prone to remember it incorrectly. You would ask yourself, *What exactly did God say?*

What if you wanted to preserve what God said to you so you'd never forget? What if you wanted to preserve it in such a way that people could have access to it long after you're gone? After all, God communicating with you would be a big deal. We wouldn't want it to be lost. How might you preserve this word from God? You would probably write it down. That sounds novel.

God spoke to you, so you are going to write it down for others. I bet whoever reads what you write is going to think to themselves at some point, *Why doesn't God just speak to me?* When might that question ever be finally satisfied? The cycle could go on forever with every person wanting a direct word from God.

I hope you're picking up what I'm putting down. The same question you have about the Bible, someone could have about your experience of God speaking to you. So it's actually better for us that the prophets and apostles of old were inspired by the Holy Spirit to record exactly what God wants for us to know today. If it were all up to our personal experience, we would be questioning it forever. And the next person to come along would require the same thing, a personal revelation from God. It's good for us to trust what God has already revealed in Scripture.

A blessing or a curse?

The Bible speaks to this. The apostle John declares a blessing for anyone who reads his letter, the book of Revelation. It's the last book of the New Testament, in terms of order, but it's also the last book that was written for the New Testament. John calls down a curse on anyone who tries to add to the words of his book (Revelation 22:18). In context, John is talking specifically about the book of Revelation. But as the last book of the New Testament, I think there is a big principle here that we all need to take to heart.

John tells us not to add anything or take anything away from God's Word (Revelation 22:18–19). God's Word includes an explanation of our world from beginning to end. Why does God need to say anything else?

A Christian author once said on social media, "Want to hear God speak to you? Read your Bible. Want to hear God speak to you audibly? Read it out loud!" If God exists, and if he's personal, and if he's revealed himself in nature, history, and Scripture, then we have all we need. Sure, our experience of hearing God speak like he spoke to Moses would be nice, but we would second-guess it forever.

The truth is, this is nothing new. The people in Moses's day felt the same way. Moses wrote the first five books of the Bible. But before he wrote any part of Scripture, it all started with God revealing himself to Moses in a burning bush. God spoke to Moses and used him as a spokesperson to the masses. Some people were jealous that Moses was the one through whom God had chosen to reveal himself.

In Numbers 12, Moses's sister, Miriam, and his brother, Aaron, confront him and ask if God has only spoken through him. Couldn't the Lord speak through them too? The answer to that is "yes" and "no." Could God speak through them? Yes. Did God speak through them? No.

If you read that chapter, you'll see that God did not approve of their questions. God chose to reveal himself through Moses. He didn't take a poll. He didn't take a survey. He didn't make sure everybody got a turn. It wasn't like modern-day, elementary-age athletic competitions. Not everyone got a divine inspiration trophy.

There's something really important for us to see here. God has chosen to reveal himself in his own way. It's not up to us. He's the authority. When we demand something other than what God has chosen, we're simply following in the footsteps of Miriam and Aaron.

Are You Disrespecting My Authority?

Scripture has authority because we believe God is its ultimate author. People sometimes misinterpret this to mean Christians literally worship the Bible. We don't. We certainly shouldn't make an idol out of a physical copy of the Bible. We are to have no idols before God, including a printed book we believe he inspired.

The Bible means so much to Christians because of what it represents. It represents the very authority of God. We worship the God described in the Bible, who has revealed himself in Scripture. Our reverence for the Bible is a reflection of our worship of God. It's the basis for how we know and serve God.

If the president of the United States sent you a personal letter, you would likely cherish it. It would be a very big deal. Even more if it contained an important message for you and others. What if the president gave you specific instructions not just for you but for your family and even your entire neighborhood? That would be weird, but what if? Maybe he'd explain how he had reasons to trust you, and there were conditions making this the best way to pass on a message for you and your community. What might you do?

You could ignore the letter, since, well, why would the president write to *you*? Maybe it's a hoax. But what if you had good reason to believe it really came from the president? What if secret service agents delivered it to your door? What if it had the presidential seal on the letterhead? If you believed it truly came from the president, you'd likely do precisely what it said. It would be unlikely that you'd ignore it or even try to edit it. You'd recognize the president has more authority than you do, and you weren't given license to change the content of his letter.

In a far greater way, if God exists, and if he has revealed himself, then we don't have the option of just ignoring his revelation. I've tried to illustrate we have good reason to trust the Bible is from God. If God used the biblical authors like Moses and Paul to write exactly what he wanted them to write without error, then we can't edit or alter it. We can't tweak it to make it better line up with how we want to live. It's an authority over us and not the other way around.

Just because we don't worship the Bible, we don't treat it lightly either. If you came to my house and found me in my front yard burning love letters from my wife, whom I love, you wouldn't think it was OK or normal because they were just letters. You'd think I'd lost my ever-loving mind. If I flippantly told you I love my wife far more than I love her letters, that would hardly change your mind. Just because I love my wife more than her letters doesn't mean I should destroy the letters. It's my love for my wife that makes me treasure what she's written to me.

The same is true with the Bible. We believe God is the ultimate authority of all things. We don't worship a book, even a book we believe is from God. Yet our belief that it's written to us from God is what makes it so important to us. That's why we begin with Scripture in forming our thoughts about God—our theology. God sets the stage for our thoughts about him.

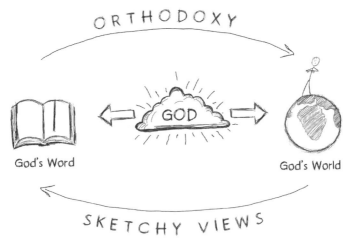

When Christians talk about the authority of the Bible, they are really talking about the authority of God. If the Bible is from God, then it represents his rule and reign over the world. But there's an important distinction to be made.

There's a difference between saying the Bible is our authority and saying someone's particular *interpretation* of the Bible is our authority. Christians can agree on the authority of the Bible even if they differ on how to best interpret it in places.

This doesn't mean everyone can come up with whatever harebrained idea they like for the Bible. There's a range of acceptable interpretations, of possible meanings, of any given text. There are common sense rules for how we interpret the Bible, a discipline called *hermeneutics*.

But even when we have the same view of the authority of Scripture, and even when we are playing by the same rules, there can still be some different interpretations. But while there may be superficial differences among Christian churches today, there is greater agreement around the major doctrines of Christianity, as expressed in many of the wonderful creeds taught throughout the history of the church. The stream of orthodoxy is deep and wide.

In this chapter we've looked more at the divine side of inspiration, at God's role in the writing of the Bible. In the next chapter, we'll take a closer look at the human side of the equation. While God inspired the words of the Bible, how exactly did the books of the Bible make their way into the form we have them today?

Questions for Reflection

1. Summarize in your own words what you believe about the Bible.
2. Why is it better for God to have revealed himself through the biblical authors than to speak directly to you today?
3. How might you respond if someone says the Bible isn't trustworthy because the people who copied the Bible made mistakes?

Oh, the Humanity!

We come to Scripture not to learn a subject
but to steep ourselves in a person.
—C. S. LEWIS

E ven if you're not a fan, I'm sure you know about the Marvel Comics superheroes. You might even have a favorite. Maybe it's Spiderman; that would be my kids' pick. There are a lot of superheroes to choose from: Black Panther, Captain Marvel, Thor, Hulk, Black Widow, Captain America, Iron Man, and the list goes on and on, including Ant Man. They're all pretty incredible, even the insect-inspired ones.

When they all come together, they're known as the Avengers. While each character has a backstory, the group as a whole has an origin story too. In the Marvel movies, it's a guy named Captain Nick Fury who originally thinks up the Avengers Initiative. The movies that follow bring together the personalities and powers of the superhero super unit, the Avengers.

This might be a helpful way to think about the Bible. Every book of the Bible has an interesting backstory. God used a bunch of authors from different walks of life. You've got Moses as a baby snatched from the Nile River. Then there's that kid who could play the harp and kill a lion with his bare hands who later became king. And there's that nasty guy named Saul who hunted Christians before turning into the world's greatest missionary.

Each author wrote in a specific time and place with a particular message. As interesting as all these stories are, there's an even bigger story about how they all came together. We often think about the Bible as if it all came about at once. Sometimes we assume there was some sort of Bible writing conference where Moses, Isaiah, Paul, James, John, and others got together to brainstorm about what to put in the Bible. Maybe they all had their own little writing cubbies. They could take occasional coffee breaks and mingle. That would be quite a sight.

There were editors, publishers, and publicists, all waiting for the final manuscript of the Holy Bible. Once the writers hit their deadlines, the books were off to the presses. Once they were printed and bound, they opened the Jerusalem Christian Bookstore and rolled out a marketing campaign. And man have they been successful! It's the greatest selling book in the history of the world.

Of course, this is not at all how the Bible came to be. It's a lot messier and more interesting. In this section, we're going to think more about the human side of the Bible equation. The Bible was written over a period of two thousand years by about forty different authors writing in three different languages. It's really unique in comparison to any other book.

Think of the Bible as an entire library of books brought together in a remarkable way. So far we've looked at how the Bible describes its authors, how they were individually moved along by the Spirit of God (*inspiration*) to write exactly what God wanted them to record without error. But when exactly did all these books known as the Bible come together?

A Tale of Two Canons

Sorry to disappoint you, but this isn't the type of cannon that pirates fired from wooden ships. Our canon has one less "n." The word *canon* here refers to an accepted body of writings. It can mean a measure for recognizing what writing or books are authoritative. The canon we're talking about is more like a ruler than a weapon.

You may have heard the term *canon* used in reference to things like the Marvel Universe or Star Wars. People will talk about the "canons of Marvel" or the "Star Wars canon" to refer to the writings or storylines considered authoritative in making sense of all their related stories.

Canon, when describing the Bible, refers to the writings the early church recognized as divinely inspired by God. It's the standard by which they judged what was to be accepted as Scripture. If a text didn't measure up, it wasn't received as having the authority of God. It could have been helpful or interesting, just not inspired by God.

The first canon we'll explore is the one believers recognized as the Old Testament. The word *testament* simply means covenant. A covenant is like a promise, a contract in which God promises to do something specific and often requires his people to do something in return.

So you can think about the Christian Bible as being divided into two sections. The bigger section is about an old covenant. The second, and shorter, part of the Bible is about a new covenant. This is a helpful way to think about Scripture—to focus on these two covenants between God and humanity.

The First Canon

The **Old Testament**, God's contract or covenant with his people, included the law and the temple, where sacrifices were made to atone for sins. The old covenant looked forward to a day when God would powerfully provide a remarkable sacrifice, a human who would die for the sins of his people (Isaiah 53).

God's people could never measure up to all God required of them in the Ten Commandments, let alone the entire law. That's why when God gave his people his law, he also gave them a tent. The tent, what the Bible calls the tabernacle, later called the temple, was the place they could go to be forgiven when they broke God's law. All these things pointed forward to a new covenant, a new testament, focused on a spectacular individual, the Messiah, whose life would fulfill the old contract and initiate a new one.

By the time Jesus was born, the books comprising the Old Testament canon were already set and recognized by those who believed in God. In fact, there was a historian named Josephus who lived around the time of Jesus who made this same point two thousand years ago: "Although such long ages have gone by, no one has dared to add anything to them [the Hebrew Scriptures], to take away anything in them, or to change anything in them."[1]

Written in Hebrew

To be clear, the Jewish believers in the time of Jesus didn't call the Scriptures the "Old Testament." They called the Scriptures the *Tanak*, a Hebrew acronym for the Law, the Prophets, and the Writings. These different books making up the Old Testament came together and were accepted by believers very early.

Those who believed in God didn't spend centuries trying to figure out what was Scripture and what wasn't. The main way they recognized an Old Testament author was writing Scripture on behalf of God was that the writer received a clear call from God to be his spokesman. That was easy enough to spot with Moses and the prophets.

God's calling for Moses was as bright as a bonfire. If there was any doubt, it was cleared up when God used Moses to perform miraculous signs in Egypt and lead God's people out of slavery. With Pharaoh's army drowned in the Red Sea, the people following in Moses's footsteps on dry land surely felt confident God was authentically talking to and through Moses.

For the most part, the Bible Jesus would have used, what Christians refer to as the Old Testament, has the exact same content our Bibles do today. The Hebrew Scriptures (or the *Tanak*) are organized differently, but they contain the same books. They merge several books together, so they have a lower number of total books, but it's the same content. One major example is the Minor Prophets (Hosea through Malachi). The *Tanak* puts all twelve minor prophets together into one book and calls it "The Book of the Twelve."

Translated into Greek

Just like we have different Bible translations today, Jesus and the disciples had a couple of options as to which Old Testament to read. Because of the military conquests

of Alexander the Great, who was a student of the philosopher Aristotle a few hundred years before Jesus was born,
the Roman world of Jesus's day was greatly influenced
by Greek culture. Sometimes people use the word *Greco-
Roman* to describe the area where Greek and Roman cultures converged.

Because Greek became the common language, and more
and more Jewish believers were speaking Greek instead of
Hebrew, the Hebrew Scriptures needed to be translated.
Followers of God have always been passionate about trans-
lating God's words into different languages so people everywhere can know of God's love. That's why they translated
the Hebrew Scriptures into the Greek language, just as they
would translate God's Word into numerous other languages
over the years.

The Greek translation of the Hebrew Scriptures is called
the *Septuagint*, which means seventy. There's a bit of a tale
about seventy scholars agreeing 100 percent about how
every word should be translated. That's really not how it
happened, as you can rarely get even a couple scholars to
completely agree on anything. Nevertheless, people still call
it by that name. You might even see it referred to by the
Roman numerals for seventy as the LXX.

When it comes to our copies of the Hebrew Scriptures,
most of them aren't all that ancient. In the last chapter we
discussed the abundance of riches we have in New Testament copies. We've got a ton of evidence! When it comes
to the Old Testament, however, most of our copies aren't
nearly as old.

For a long time, the best Old Testament copies dated
from the Middle Ages, hundreds of years after the originals
were written. That remained the case until the mid-1940s.
As the story goes, a shepherd boy goofing around near
some caves, not far from the city of Jerusalem, accidentally

discovered a hidden treasure of old manuscripts, including a bunch of ancient copies of the Old Testament.

This led to a lot of people digging around and turning up ancient copies of the Hebrew Scriptures dating back hundreds of years before Jesus was born. In comparing the Old Testament copies from the Middle Ages with these older copies, now called the Dead Sea Scrolls, we can see how what God originally communicated to the Old Testament authors had been faithfully preserved and passed down through the years. It's remarkable how God's revelation has withstood the test of time.

You should probably know that there's also a group of additional books that some Bibles include with the Old Testament, particularly Roman Catholic Bibles. These extra books are called the *Apocrypha*. You may have heard of them, especially if you have a Catholic friend or family member.

The Apocrypha is a collection of writings penned after the Old Testament canon was completed and before the New Testament was written. This is fittingly referred to as the "intertestamental" period." The Apocrypha was not written in Hebrew, like the Old Testament, but in Greek.

There is good evidence in the history of the church that these books were not considered part of the Old Testament canon from the earliest time. That's why Protestants —Christians who aren't members of the Catholic Church— don't place them in their Bibles. While the Apocrypha might include interesting stories or insights, it does not carry the authority of inspiration by God.

Waiting for more

As we noted at the beginning of the chapter, the old covenant or Old Testament, points to something else, to something new. It predicts a new covenant. These two covenants are linked together in a remarkable way. The prophet Jeremiah says this:

> "Look, the days are coming"—this is the LORD's declaration—"when I will make a new covenant with the house of Israel and with the house of Judah. This one will not be like the covenant I made with their ancestors on the day I took them by the hand to lead them out of the land of Egypt—my covenant that they broke even though I am their master"—the LORD's declaration. "Instead, this is the covenant I will make with the house of Israel after those days"—the LORD's declaration. "I will put my teaching within them and write it on their hearts. I will be their God, and they will be my people." (Jeremiah 31:31–33)

By the time we get to the end of the era of the prophets, the end of our Old Testament, things are bleak. God had removed his Spirit from the temple as a sign of judgment. He was no longer communicating to his people through the prophets.

This was the time between the testaments. There were four centuries between the close of the Old Testament and the birth of Jesus. Though God was never really gone, his Spirit wasn't visibly at work in the midst of his people as before. During this period, God wasn't talking to his people. It was a spiritually dark time.

Thankfully, this isn't the end of the story, and this wasn't a time entirely devoid of hope. There was still the expectation that when God's chosen one, the Messiah, finally came onto the scene, there would be a powerful outpouring of God's Spirit. Then God would again speak to his people. With the coming of the Messiah there would be additions to Scripture.

In other words, the Old Testament anticipated the coming of the new covenant, the coming of the New Testament.

The Second Canon

The opening of the Gospel of John powerfully connects to the beginning of the Old Testament: "In the beginning" (John 1:1). Those are the exact same words Moses pens to begin Genesis. The apostle John continues, "In the beginning was the Word . . . The Word became flesh and dwelt among us" (1:1, 14). The old covenant begins with the God who made all things. The new covenant begins with the birth of Jesus, God in the flesh, the one who came to make all things new.

Jesus loved the Hebrew Scriptures, the Old Testament. He constantly points back to them. And Jesus commissioned the New Testament, commanding his disciples to take his message to the world. He promises them the Holy Spirit to guide them into remembering and teaching everything he taught (Matthew 28; John 14). Again, this is what Christians are referring to when we say the Bible is inspired by God. This is what I mean when I say Jesus commissioned the New Testament.

When it was written

We've seen how there were hundreds of years of silence between God's inspiration of the Old Testament and the New Testament. But how long did it take for the New Testament to be written once it got started? How long did it take believers to understand and accept that it too, like the Old Testament, was inspired Scripture from God? How long do you think it should have taken for the twenty-seven books of the New Testament to be written and then recognized by the early church?

Well, for starters, it didn't take long for God to keep his promise of sending the Spirit. The Spirit was recorded as coming in the opening chapters of the book of Acts, which record the origin and exponential growth of the Christian church. Just like the prophet Joel had predicted, God's Spirit was doing a new thing (Joel 2:28–29).

From the earliest days of the church, Christians were persecuted, marginalized, and scattered. These first disciples were followers of a Jewish carpenter who was executed as an enemy of the state. Do you really think they could advertise their writings or get together for a big conference to publish all the letters the apostles were writing? Of course not.

The stories about Jesus and his teachings first spread by word of mouth. A lot of people at this time were illiterate, so this was the best way to spread the gospel. Followers of Jesus were excited to share the news of what they'd seen and heard with their own eyes, even at the risk of their own lives.

The main requirement for a New Testament author was that he was either an apostle or someone in close relationship with an apostle. An apostle was someone who was called and sent by Jesus himself. This is similar to the Old Testament requirement for a biblical author to be a person directly called by God.

Over time, God guided the apostles and their close associates, to write inspired accounts of Jesus's life. The Spirit moved these men as they wrote, reminding them of the works and words of Jesus, while keeping them from error. As the message of Jesus spread far and wide, the apostles also wrote letters, what we sometimes call "epistles," explaining how churches should conduct themselves and believe and practice.

Most of the New Testament books are epistles or letters to churches. That should give us some insight into just how important the church is in God's work on earth. Even the last book of the Bible is no exception. The book of Revelation begins with seven letters to seven churches where people were being persecuted. It records the end of human history when Jesus returns to make all things new.

This is a bit of an overview, but the question remains: When did believers recognize the letters making up the New Testament? Again, how long did it take for Christians to publicly acknowledge what they believed was Scripture?

Theologian Norman Geisler says, "The New Testament was written between about A.D. 50 and 90, and all major branches of Christianity accept its twenty-seven books as inspired and canonical."[2] Let's unpack that timeline a bit more. The apostle John wrote the book of Revelation, the last book of the Bible, toward the end of the first century. That's approximately sixty years after Jesus's resurrection. By the turn of the first century, God's Spirit had inspired the apostles and their close associates to write all the books of the New Testament. That's when the writing of the New Testament was completed.

You might think that answers our question about when we got the New Testament. In a sense it does. We have a general timeline for when the New Testament authors finished their writing. But you might still be curious about how long it took this new movement of young, persecuted churches sprawling away from Jerusalem, what we now call Christianity, to recognize and promote the canon of the New Testament.

When it was recognized

Today authors will often have a release party when they publish a new book. I'll probably have some kind of party for this book when it finally comes out. That means I'll likely take my family out to eat at Cracker Barrel or some really expensive place like that and hold up a copy and say, "Look kids!" and they'll all try to act impressed. You're invited, by the way. I hope you like good pancakes and bad coffee. See you there.

Do you think there would have been a New Testament release party when most of the authors of the New Testament were tortured and killed for their beliefs? How might that have looked or taken place?

Sometimes skeptics will suggest that no one made a formal list of the books that should be included in the New Testament until a guy named Athanasius did in the fourth century. That's three hundred years after John finished Revelation. Should we throw up our hands and conclude that the New Testament really can't be from God if it took that long for there to be a release party?

No. For starters, it's clear the church recognized the New Testament canon long before Athanasius. The fledgling churches of the second century, as they slowly received handmade copies of various portions of the New Testament, were quicker than some skeptics realize in demonstrating their acceptance. Though we don't have an early public release party, we do have evidence as to what these early Christian leaders saw as inspired Scripture, particularly when they were trying to defend what they believed against false teachings—what we've described as sketchy views.

For example, there was a guy named Marcion who was born about ten years before the apostle John wrote the book of Revelation. He was not a big fan of connecting the New Testament to the Old Testament. In fact, he wanted to get rid of a whole lot of the Bible, mainly the entire Old Testament. He promoted ditching the *Tanak* in its entirety and keeping only an edited version of the Gospel of Luke and some of Paul's letters. Marcion's Bible would be radically smaller than ours.

Marcion was considered a heretic. He had some really sketchy views of God that outlived him and are even still around in different forms today. We can tell a lot about what Christians saw as New Testament Scripture by how they responded to the sketchy views of Marcion.

There was one church leader named Tertullian who was born shortly before Marcion's death. As Tertullian came of age, he challenged Marcion's students, who were continuing to promote a very different version of Scripture and ultimately a sketchy view of God. In his response to Marcion's views, Tertullian quoted from every New Testament author except James. Though Tertullian was not trying to give us an exhaustive list of which books comprised the New Testament canon, it's clear from his response to Marcion that he was drawing from the breadth of New Testament writers and writings.

Tertullian was not alone in his promotion of the New Testament authors. Around the same time, another leader named Origin went as far as to say that God had inspired twenty-seven books in the New Testament, what he described as twenty-seven trumpets. That's the same number we have in our New Testament books today. Again, this all illustrates how the church recognized the canon of the New Testament at a very early date, even though a formal list wasn't released until the fourth century.

That brings us to Athanasius and his New Testament release party. In AD 367, Athanasius outlined all the books we find in our English Bibles today. But long before this, it was clear Christian leaders recognized the New Testament authors and their writings as coming from God. They saw their role more as recognizing the canon, and less as making it.

Though there were some disputes here or there, most of the books of the New Testament were universally received by Christian churches and leaders at an early date. God gave the Church all it needed to thrive in a fallen world.

A Sufficiently Simple Solution to the Bible

As a young boy I remember seeing an action movie where the hero had a survival knife. I thought it was the coolest thing in the world. From that moment, I was determined to get one. I wanted to be Rambo.

One side of his blade was sharp, and the other had jagged teeth to saw stuff. The end of the handle had a compass as a lid, which, if turned and unscrewed, opened a compartment in the handle. All kinds of stuff were inside, like matches to start a fire, a flint to sharpen the blade, some fishing line, and a hook. I was convinced, if I had a knife like this, I could survive anything. I could conquer the world!

It had everything you needed to make it in the wild. Unlike the hero in the movie, I lacked a whole lot of muscle and know how. But I did eventually get the knife. I just never got myself lost enough to make good use of it, which is probably good. I'm not sure it really had all I would personally need to survive. These days I have a hard time making it through my morning without coffee.

The survival knife was marketed as having all the survival essentials. That's how advertising works. There's usually some measure of exaggeration, and there's always a pitch. "Buy this and you won't need anything ever again!" I'm sure you've heard a line like that before.

The Bible makes a similar claim. The apostle Peter says God has given us all we need "for life and godliness" (2 Peter 1:3). Is this an exaggerated claim? Is it just another marketing pitch? Is the Bible really sufficient? Yes and no. Let me explain.

I'll start with the "no." The Bible is not saying it gives us all we need to learn how to change the oil in our car. The Bible is not saying it gives us all we need to operate on someone's brain. To do either of those things, we're going to need more than the Bible.

But what about "yes"? What is Peter's point in telling us we have all we need for life and godliness? Here's a hint: it probably relates to how we can live a life pleasing to God. When it comes to brain surgery, you need to go to medical school for a long time. If you want to work on automobiles, you need training in mechanics.

Medical or mechanical training, surprising as this might be, won't make you a more faithful follower of Jesus. Sure, there are principles of discipline and diligence that can be applied to your life as a Christian. But studying neuroscience or auto mechanics isn't going to increase your knowledge of God.

Let me illustrate it this way: Three of my four children have an identical genetic disease. Their bodies are unable to properly metabolize. They can't break down the fat in the food they eat, or even process body fat if they go a long time without food. That means if they get sick and are unable to hold down food, their bodies are at risk. It's like driving a car with no gas in the tank. They won't make it very far. They can experience seizures and even risk death.

It's not uncommon during flu season for us to spend a few days in the hospital. If one of our kids gets a stomach bug, we typically pack a bag and get ready to go. I've never taken my kids to the emergency room and asked them to be treated using only the Bible. I've never told our geneticist she can only use treatments that are clearly found in Scripture. That would be wrongheaded and poor parenting.

While medicine and science can and have saved my kids' lives, these things can't tell my kids how to pursue a life worth living. Where can they discover that? How can they have a relationship with God? Where can they go when they desperately need forgiveness? Where can they find purpose? How might they find direction when everything seems to be spinning around them?

They can find answers to these questions in the Bible. God has given them all they need to live a meaningful life that's pleasing to him. They have all they need in the Bible to know how to succeed in this life and prepare for the next. That's not to say it has all they will ever need to know, but it has all the most important things. That's how the Bible is sufficient.

In the sixteenth century, the German theologian Martin Luther famously challenged the religious leaders of his day for requiring more out of believers than what was found in Scripture. He'd had enough of people adding to the Bible, so he finally protested. He nailed a list of challenges (the Ninety-five Theses) regarding these extra requirements to a church door in his town in Germany, marking the beginning of the Protestant Reformation. He argued that Christians should solely rely upon Scripture as their ultimate authority. Luther believed the Bible was sufficient for what we are to believe and teach about God. That doesn't mean you can't learn all kinds of stuff from sources outside the Bible. You can and should.

I have the unique privilege of teaching students who are going to be nurses, educators, pharmacists, and a whole lot more. I encourage them to pursue their professions with excellence, to do it for the glory of God. But no matter what or where they learn, or from whom, they should always come back to Scripture as their sufficient and authoritative guide for living a life pleasing to God.

Take and Read

All this talk about the authority and sufficiency of the Bible might make you a little nervous. The Bible is a big book. And not all of it is easy to understand. What are you to do? Let me offer some encouragement. You can spend your entire life reading the Bible and never master the whole thing. That's OK. You have to start somewhere.

You'll never be able to check off your need for the Bible on some to-do list. You'll never graduate from the Bible in this lifetime. So don't let its enormity keep you from taking the first step. It's been said that a journey of a thousand miles begins with one step. So take the first step.

Another famous church leader named Augustine once recalled hearing a voice directing to him Scripture with the words, "take and read." I hope you hear that same message in one way or another. Take and read. The Bible can change your life. Reading the Bible is necessary to grow your spiritual life. It has all you need to grow in your relationship with God.

God inspired the Bible in such a way that it's accessible to everyone, normal people like you and me. Maybe that's why God used real humans to write his message. Its central message is simple and clear.

That's why it's helpful to keep in mind the two banks on both sides of the orthodox view of the Bible. There's the divine side, where we see God as the ultimate author, and the human side, where God used human authors to write exactly what he wanted without error, and for the church to recognize what was inspired by God. The result? The Bible contains exactly what God wants you to know about him, his world, and your place in it.

In addition to all that, the Bible teaches Christians that they have God's Spirit in them to help them better understand and apply Scripture. That means you're not alone. And you have a lot of help from other Christians too, to help you make sense of things.

The Bible is so amazing that you can spend your entire life learning the original languages in which it was written (Hebrew, Greek, and Aramaic), studying the oldest of manuscripts, reading and thinking about every verse, and still just scratch the surface on all Scripture teaches about God. Yet the Bible is so simple that a young person can read it, understand it, and flourish in their relationship with God. While it's helpful to have Bible scholars who can shed light on difficult passages, every believer can pick up their Bible for themselves and grow in their walk with God.

Questions for Reflection

1. How would you summarize the way God brought the Old and New Testaments together?
2. How is the Bible sufficient for your life?
3. What are some ways you can plan to study God's Word every day?
4. Do you have to be a scholar to understand the Bible?

God

What's the Matter?

The riddles of God are more satisfying
than the solutions of man.
—G. K. CHESTERTON

On our journey so far, we've navigated the bends and rapids of the doctrine of Scripture. We've looked at how God used human authors to write exactly what he wanted so we can know more about who he is. We've also talked about reasons to trust Scripture. Now let's look to Scripture to see what we are to believe about God. This is called the *doctrine of God*.

The stream of orthodoxy is framed by two rich biblical realities. On one bank we see that there is only one God, or what we will call the oneness of God. On the other bank, we see that God exists as three persons, what we call the Trinity. It can be a bit confusing, I know. It is, after all, a mystery. What did you expect?

Nonetheless, these are the borders through which the orthodox view of God flows. That God is one and that he is a Trinity frame our beliefs about God. This chapter will focus on God's oneness, while the next will look at how this one God exists as Father, Son, and Spirit.

God Is

Belief in God is basic. The default human condition is religious. In contrast, atheism is a learned perspective. Just read any of the polls on this topic. Studies consistently show the overwhelming majority of people around the world believe there is something more than mere nature. All of us are looking for answers to the biggest questions of all. That tends to make us open to belief in God.

Nonetheless, throughout much of human history, a lot of intellectuals have gravitated toward the view that the world is all there is and that it is eternal. Especially for those who want to deny the existence of a Creator, denying the universe had a beginning is a common first move. If the universe doesn't have a beginning, then we don't have to explain where (or who) it came from.

From as far back as the Greek philosopher Aristotle, who lived over three hundred years before Jesus was born, all the way up to Albert Einstein, many great thinkers have believed that the world doesn't have a beginning. Aristotle believed some outside source must exist, some unmoved mover or first cause. But he, like Einstein, accepted as certain that the universe has always existed.

Lots of people have thought this way—except for those who believed God had revealed something about the world, namely, that it had a beginning. Jews and Christians have always believed the world was created at some point in the past. They didn't hold that view because of science, but because of Scripture. Nevertheless, science has turned out to support the biblical view.

Einstein reluctantly accepted the universe had a beginning.[1] His theory of general relativity pointed to a beginning. At first, he tried to avoid this by adjusting the details, but in time he finally gave in and followed the evidence where it led—to a point in the past when the world came into being.

In addition to Einstein's theory, there has been scientific evidence pointing to a beginning as well. Nobel Prize winning scientist Arno Penzias codiscovered material evidence, a kind of canopy at the edge of our expanding universe left over from the explosive creation event. When asked by the *New York Times* about his shocking discovery, Penzias told the journalist that what he found is exactly the kind of thing that should have been expected if one had nothing to go on but the writings of Moses.[2]

Again, those who believe that God exists, that he is personal, and that he has revealed himself, have always held the position that the world has a beginning. This distinction between Creator and created is plain enough in Scripture, quite literally, from the very beginning. That God existed eternally before the world existed—before he created the world—is the starting point of the Bible.

Genesis begins by explaining the origin of our world with no argument or explanation for how God came to be. The teaching throughout Scripture is that God has eternally existed and has no cause outside himself. "Before the mountains were born," the psalmist says of God, "before you gave birth to the earth and the world, from eternity to eternity, you are God" (Psalm 90:2). This is the Christian elephant, the belief in the existence of a personal God who has revealed himself.

The God of Nature

All this leads us to an interesting argument for God's existence. It goes a little like this: Everything that begins to exist has a cause. The universe began to exist. Therefore, the universe has a cause. Pretty interesting, isn't it?

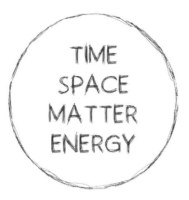

Before we look at it in more depth, let's begin by taking note of what this argument does not claim. It does not say that everything has a cause. That would mean that God must have a cause, which doesn't line up with how God has revealed himself. Because God is self-existent, what theologians describe as *Divine Aseity*, he is without a cause. God exists by himself, without our help.

The apostle Paul highlights this reality in Romans. This rich theological letter makes a stark transition from glorious truths about God in chapters 1–11, to how the believer should apply them in chapter 12 and following. Before Paul makes that transition from truth to application, he asks three rhetorical questions at the end of Romans 11:

> Oh, the depth of the riches
> and the wisdom and the knowledge of God!
> How unsearchable his judgments
> and untraceable his ways!
> For who has known the mind of the Lord?
> Or who has been his counselor?
> And who has ever given to God,
> that he should be repaid?
> For from him and through him
> and to him are all things.

To him be the glory forever.
Amen. (Romans 11:33–36)

I like to think of this passage as Paul's commencement address for his theology students. They've labored through eleven chapters of rich theology. They are about to graduate to practical matters. Before Paul lets them move on, he asks them to consider three questions: (1) Who has known God's mind? (2) Who has been God's counselor? (3) To whom is God indebted? The answer to each of these questions is, No one.

God is eternal and self-existent. He has no cause. He has no need. Nothing created him, and nothing sustains him. Our world points to his gracious act of creation. He didn't need to make us to fill some deficiency on his part. And the way creation points to him offers a powerful argument.

So if the universe had a beginning, and therefore has a cause, then we can start to reason about what that cause is like.[3] We can describe the universe as consisting of time, space, matter, and energy. Even though these terms can be difficult to define, even among scientists and philosophers, they are often used to summarize what the world is. So whatever the cause of the universe is, its cause existed before it and without it. That means the cause of the universe must be outside of time, space, matter, and energy.

Even if you don't like philosophical arguments, please stick with me. What would it mean for something to exist outside of time? If something is outside of time, it would have to be timeless or eternal. Does that sound like God? A little, doesn't it? We're getting closer, aren't we?

If something exists outside of space, then it's a bit more complicated to understand. You might immediately think about something in outer space. I get it. That's not what we're talking about though. Outer space is still space; it's just beyond the earth's atmosphere. We're talking about something that exists without any spatial limits or features.

There was a popular song in the nineties where the artist said he wished he was taller, and he wished he was a baller. I relate. I would wish for both of those things too. I take after my short Italian mother. But no matter how much I wish, I'm not getting any taller. I have spatial features. I'm under six foot tall. I can't change that. I also have a big nose, but let's not focus on that. And I have spatial limitations, like I can't be in two places at once.

God doesn't have spatial features, like a height or weight. He also doesn't have spatial limitations. He can be in different places at the same time. In fact, Christians believe he is present everywhere at the same time. The word we use for that is *omnipresent*. Look at how this psalmist talks about God:

> Where can I go to escape your Spirit?
> Where can I flee from your presence?
> If I go up to heaven, you are there;
> if I make my bed in Sheol, you are there.
> If I fly on the wings of the dawn
> and settle down on the western horizon,
> even there your hand will lead me;
> your right hand will hold on to me.
> If I say, "Surely the darkness will hide me,
> and the light around me will be night"
> —even the darkness is not dark to you.
> The night shines like the day;
> darkness and light are alike to you. (Psalm 139:7–12)

So far we've seen that if the universe had a beginning, its source must be eternal (outside time) and without spatial features or limitations (*omnipresent*). Additionally, what might it mean for the cause of the universe to be outside of matter? It would mean this source, or the cause, of the universe is immaterial or spirit. Does that sound like God?

The apostle Paul describes God as "eternal, immortal, invisible, the only God" (1 Timothy 1:17). Jesus described God the Father as spirit (John 4:24). That's why the children of Israel were commanded not to make an idol, any kind of graven image of God (Exodus 20:4). God doesn't have a physical image. He's immaterial and outside of matter.

That's why all this talk about God not having any physical dimensions or limitations makes the incarnation, the birth of Jesus, when the Word became flesh, so fantastic. In Jesus, this invisible, eternal, and all-powerful God is now made visible (John 1:14; Galatians 4:7). The apostle John sums it up like this, "No one has ever seen God. The one and only Son, who is himself God and is at the Father's side —he has revealed him" (John 1:18).

I think of that first Christmas day when the King of Kings was born in Bethlehem. Think about it. The power that created the world, now displayed in seven to eight pounds of human flesh wrapped in a first-century diaper. It's like what the genie says about living in a lamp in Disney's movie *Aladdin*, "Phenomenal cosmic power. Itty bitty living space!"[4] The only way we can know the Creator of the world is if he were to step into our world in a way we could know him personally.

The final description of our world for us to consider here is that of energy. If our world of time, space, matter, and energy was created, this means there is an immensely powerful cause behind creation. The theological term for this attribute of God is *omnipotence*. Our world points to an eternal, omnipresent, and omnipotent Spirit, whom we call God. All of reality is pointing to him.

The philosopher Francis Bacon once said, "A little philosophy inclineth man's mind to atheism, but depth in philosophy bringeth men's minds about to religion."[5] If you
think deeply about the world—that it even exists and had
a beginning—it'll direct your attention to the presence and
power of God. In sum, the cause of the universe sounds a
whole lot like the God of the Bible.

The Nature of God

Everything we've covered so far in the previous paragraphs
point to what theologians refer to as God's *transcendence*.
God exists apart from time, space, matter, and energy. He
isn't contained in the world like a lightning bug you might
catch in summertime and stick in a mason jar. By defini-
tion, God is a being who exists before and beyond our natural world.

God has eternally existed and needs nothing and no
one. The whole universe could cease to exist, and God
would still be God without being reduced to something less
in any way. God is completely independent.

That can be hard for us to take in. That's OK. There's only one God, so trying to make him fit any kind of comparison can be, well, impossible. It's hard to think about someone being self-existing because our days are mostly filled with created things. How can we imagine someone being self-dependent when everything we see and touch today will be dependent on something or someone else?

You're dependent too, more than you might realize. If you lost access to food and water, you wouldn't live long. If you lost access to air, you'd die even quicker. You get the point. There are many things your existence depends on, including your parents, without whom there wouldn't be a you. So if God is so different from everything we know, how can we really ever know anything about God?

We've considered how the Bible explains that we know there's a God simply by being human. God made you to know he is real. That's why the apostle Paul says you immediately perceive his eternal power and divine nature when you look at the world (Romans 1). But just how much can we learn about this eternal, all-powerful, everywhere-present Spirit that created the world?

If God isn't in any way dependent on the world he created, if he is outside of time, space, matter, and energy, how can we ever hope to know anything about him? If God is transcendent, is he out of our reach? The short answer to that is "yes." We can't reach him on our own. If he exists, and if he's the sort of being that's outside the natural world, then our getting to know him would completely, 100 percent, be up to him and not us.

C. S. Lewis used a literary illustration in his essay "Is Theology Poetry?" to explain the way we relate to God For his example, he used the great Italian poet Dante Alighieri, who wrote an epic poem called *The Divine Comedy*.[6] You've probably heard of it. It's not the kind of comedy you might think of. It's a serious work, not really that funny at all. It's all about God and eternity and what matters most for humans in life and death.

As a writer, Dante created the world within his story. That's what fiction authors do. The better the author, the better the world. Think about J. R. R. Tolkien and his world of the Shire and Middle Earth. Or maybe you're a Harry Potter fan. If so, what images come to your mind when you think of Hogwarts? The authors of your favorite stories put a lot of time and thought into making them.

Generally speaking, you won't find any physical evidence for an author inside their story. In one sense, the worlds they create owe their existence entirely to their authors. For example, we wouldn't have Hogwarts without J. K. Rowling. We wouldn't have Middle Earth without J. R. R. Tolkien. But we don't find these authors themselves anywhere inside their stories—sitting at a table at Hogwarts or roaming Middle Earth. The authors exist apart from the worlds they created.

Yet there are some stories where their authors intentionally write themselves into the plot. C. S. Lewis pointed this out in the writings of Dante. In his famous story *The Divine Comedy*, Dante inserted himself into the story line. Dante made himself a character in his epic poem. As C. S. Lewis explained, this sheds a little light on how we can get to know the Creator of our world.

If we are ever to know the eternal, all-powerful, everywhere-present Spirit whom we call God, it won't be through any effort of our own. We're like characters in Dante's play. The only way to know Dante is if he were to write himself in. Christians believe God has done something very similar.

To begin with, God is the main subject of the first chapter of Genesis. In one sense, he has clearly been part of the story from the beginning. But Adam and Eve choose to rebel against God. The first couple were exiled from the garden of Eden. The Old Testament is peppered with examples of God showing up in different ways to relate to the characters in his story, the true story of the world in which we live.

God speaks through the burning bush to Moses. God later crafts the stone tablets with the Ten Commandments, before Moses gets angry and breaks them (Exodus 32:18–19). God speaks through the prophets. And God even writes a message on a wall in Daniel 5 (which is where we get the expression "the handwriting is on the wall"). But all those things were pointing to the big thing, the event where God would enter his created world in a powerful way.

The author of our story, God, has written himself into the plot. He has come near so that we can know him. This is what theologians refer to as *immanence*. God is both transcendent, existing outside of time, but also immanent, having entered time.

Christmas really is a celebration of God's immanence, his coming near. The birth of Jesus is literally celebrated around the world. It's the defining date that divides human history. The birth of Jesus is called the incarnation, a word that means God in the flesh. The immaterial Creator has entered the material world he created.

Jesus Is the Key

We've seen how the mere fact that our material world began to exist points to a source outside itself, an ultimate cause we call God. This timeless, powerful, omnipresent, Spirit is transcendent. That means God exists outside the world. He is not the sum total of the created world. He is not spread across the universe like a vapor. He is not in everything. He exists outside time, space, matter, and energy.

While all that shows we can't get to God on our own, the good news is that he came to us. God reveals himself as an act of his love for his creation. "For God loved the world in this way," John tells us, "He gave his one and only Son . . ." (John 3:16).

As we've seen, this God is not only transcendent, he's also *immanent*. God exists outside our world, but for love's sake, he entered the world he created. This is the core of Christian theology. This is who we believe God is. This is what we believe God is like. Of course, the Christian believes more than this, but never less. In other words, if you want to know what God is like, look at Jesus.

I once heard a story of a dying soldier who asked a minister attending to his final moments, "Is God like Jesus?" That might strike you as a weird question. Most of the time we think about it in the opposite direction: Is Jesus like God? But John's gospel tells us that it is through the incarnation, through God taking human flesh, that we can understand God.

This soldier wanted to know if the God he was about to face after death was like the amazing person of Jesus. It's a powerful question. He was looking in the right direction. If you want to know what God is like, look to Jesus. What is God like? He is love. He is mercy. He is truth. He is perfect justice. He is willing to suffer and die for his people so they might have life. That's what God is like.

Look at the Jesus of the New Testament. He is a friend of outcasts. He comforts the broken. He defends those who can't protect themselves. Jesus compassionately converses with the woman at the well, a woman who had been rejected and dejected (John 4). Jesus meets her at her point of need and offers her water, which will cause her to never thirst again—if she will receive it. That's what God is like.

In anguish and pain, hanging naked on a tree, beaten and bloody, spikes through his wrists and ankles, a crown of thorns piercing his temple, Jesus has compassion on an unnamed thief who dared to believe. Jesus promises him paradise. That's what God is like.

After Jesus rose from the dead, he comforts the disciples who abandoned him in the midst of their fear. He pursues Peter who denied him three times, giving him three opportunities to say, "I love you, Jesus." That's what God is like.

If you want to know what God is like, look at Jesus. That's something worth thinking about. Whenever you question something in the Bible that's hard to understand, start with the simple things that are the clearest. Let your view of God begin and end with Jesus. Return to him often and always. If you want to know what God is like, look to Jesus.

Jesus is the key to making sense of God. But that raises a whole lot of questions, doesn't it? How do we make sense of there being one God, but we talk about God the Father, God the Son, and God the Spirit? How can God still be one when he seems to be three? I'm glad you asked. (Turn to the next chapter.)

Questions for Reflection

1. How does the fact that the material world had a beginning point to God?
2. What can we know about God by looking at Jesus?
3. Do you know someone who doesn't believe in God? Take time now to pray for them to come to understand the truth of the gospel.

Saint Patrick on Bad Analogies

Some things have to be believed to be seen.
—MADELEINE L'ENGLE

There are about a million ways to get God wrong. Getting God right, on the other hand, can be a tricky endeavor. The history of the Christian church makes this pretty clear. You can find a lot of thinkers who went off the rails in their attempts to explain God. Sometimes even good people are rather proficient in discovering bad ways to talk about God.

Take Saint Patrick, for example. No, he's not just a mythological figure. I'm not sure if he ever pinched anyone for not wearing green. He wasn't a leprechaun.

He was a real-life person who was kidnapped from Britain as a teenager and sent into slavery in Ireland. He later escaped and was reunited with his family. But, as providence would see fit, as an adult, he moved back to Ireland to share the Christian faith in the land where he was once held captive. Today he is considered the apostle to Ireland.

It's thought Saint Patrick used the shamrock to explain the Trinity. It makes sense. It's just one clover, but it has three leaves. Of course, if you're really lucky, you can find one with four leaves. Who knows? Maybe Patrick used that to talk about the four Gospels.

An analogy is a comparison between two things for the purpose of explanation. You start with something familiar, in this case a shamrock, then you explain something unfamiliar, like the Trinity. Here's the problem: it doesn't work. Every analogy for God starts to unravel rather quickly.

Since there's only one God, there's nothing you can compare him to. There's nothing entirely like him. When you say, "God is kind of like this or that," you've already committed a "categorical error" of one kind or another. God exists in a category of his own. There's nothing else in his category.

By "categorical error," here's what I mean: There are two big categories into which everything that exists can be placed. There are things that *aren't* created. Only God fits there. Then there are things that *are* created. Everything outside of God falls into that bucket.

When you take a created thing and compare it to an uncreated thing, it's a categorical error. It doesn't quite work. This isn't to say there aren't some ways analogies can serve a limited purpose. We just need to use caution and recognize their limitations.

So, in addition to being remembered for an excuse to drink more than one should in celebration of his legacy every March, Saint Patrick illustrates a sketchy way to explain God. That doesn't mean he was a sketchy person. Again, it's just that every analogy you come up with to explain God is going to be limited. If you take any analogy to its logical conclusion, it will fall short of God's glory.

It reminds me of commercials advertising the latest televisions. They boast about a superior display and sound, but everything they show to impress you is coming through your own screen. Whatever you see or hear is channeled through the television you already own. There's really no way they can show you how their television is superior to yours when all they have to work with is your screen and speakers. I remember thinking one time when I saw a commercial like that, *Wow that does have a clear picture!* Of course, I immediately laughed at myself when it occurred to me that the picture of their display was coming through my display. That's when I thought, *Hey, my screen is pretty good. I don't need a new television after all!* I guess their marketing kind of backfired.

Here's another example. I'm old enough to remember black and white television sets. We had one at our house, though we also had a color set in our living room. If you were to watch a full-color movie on the black and white set, it would just come out in black and white. Because the black and white set doesn't have an option to project color, no matter what signal is pumped into it, it's just going to produce varying shades of gray.

These examples illustrate the limitations we have in trying to picture God. We inevitably end up relying on language that's common to us, even though God is far from common. We're doing the best we can, but we're trying to project a full-color picture on a black and white television set. That's why any analogy, like what Patrick allegedly used, is going to fall short. Though what we're trying to describe is in full color, all we end up sharing is black and white. Even this analogy falls short, doesn't it?

A Divine Kidnapping

Speaking of television, imagine if you voluntarily gave up all your forms of entertainment and distraction for an entire week. Imagine being confined to a comfortable room with no screens. All you get for the entire week is a Bible and a notebook. You would have all your meals and plenty of drinks to keep you hydrated. You would be kept perfectly comfortable.

In this scenario, you would have no other responsibilities for an entire week but to read the Bible from cover to cover and write down observations about God. From morning until evening, you would just be reading large sections of Scripture from Genesis to Revelation. You might be surprised to learn that you could read through the Bible more than once in this week.

The only thing you'd be expected to produce during the week would be a short summary of all your observations about God. What do you think you'd come up with? I think I have a pretty good idea. You'd end up with something dangerously close to what we call the *doctrine of the Trinity*. Here's why I think that would be the case.

You would start in Genesis and notice that God created the world (Genesis 1:1). But then you might see in the verses that follow that God's Spirit is now involved in the world (Genesis 1:2). Then you'd likely scratch your head when you realize God is talking to himself when he says, "Let us make man in our image" (Genesis 1:26).

In reading through Exodus, you'd see the clear emphasis that there's only one God (Exodus 6). You'd likely write down something about how important it seems that God's people recognize there's only one God and that they not have any other gods besides him (Deuteronomy 6:4). You might even write down, "There is only one God."

In working on your summary statement, you'd probably look back at your notes from Genesis and think, *Well, there's something odd about this one God. He talks to himself. His Spirit seems to be pretty important. What's up with that?*

That's not all. I'd imagine you'd pick up on the powerful promises and predictions that God would send someone to deliver his people, who is often called the Messiah. This promise shows up as early as Genesis 3:15, when God tells the serpent that one of Eve's future children will defeat evil.

So your summary would include this one God who talks to himself, who has a powerful Spirit, and who has promised a chosen one, a Messiah, who will rule forever. What do you make of all that? We haven't even made it to the New Testament yet! This one God is kind of different, isn't he? He doesn't fit our categories.

As we've described, the only way we can know the transcendent source of creation is if he comes to us. We can't understand him on our own. That's exactly why Jesus says he came to the world.

While being held hostage to study the Bible, you'd see in the Gospels how Jesus claims to be God in a number of ways. He says he existed before Abraham was born (John 8:58). He claims to be equal with God the Father (John 14:9–11). He does stuff only God was supposed to do, like forgiving sin (Luke 7:48). And it's clear the apostles believed him to be God since they claimed he was eternal, created all things, and sustains the world (John 1:1–4; Colossians 1:16–17).

The Biblical Data

What do you do with all this stuff about God? How do you make sense of him? How do you think about and talk about God without violating what's revealed in the Bible? How do you avoid sketchy views?

You might write down something like, "There's only one God, but the Holy Spirit and Jesus seem like they are God too." You might even go so far as to say, "It seems like the Father, the Son, and the Spirit are all God." Having taught enough students over the years, I've learned this much—the doctrine of the Trinity makes sense of a lot of stuff. To put it another way, it's hard to make sense of what's going on with God in the Bible without the doctrine of the Trinity.

Another way of thinking about the Trinity is not just how we might make sense of it, but what does it help make sense of? First, and most importantly, it makes sense of the biblical data. I'm convinced it would be very difficult to make sense of a lot of biblical passages without the doctrine of the Trinity. In other words, it's the key to unlocking the door behind which we can glimpse the mystery of God in the Bible.

Uncreated

Throughout the history of the church, there have been several sketchy views about God, and a lot of them relate to getting the Trinity wrong. For example, a guy named Arius was convinced Jesus was a created person and not fully God. One of the most famous verses in the Bible, John 3:16, says "God so loved the world, that he gave his only begotten son" (KJV). Arius understood the word *begotten* to mean created. Does *begotten* mean created?

What do we do with that? If you were to go back to the first chapter of this book and review the method I outlined for doing theology, you'd know that you should let the clearer passages shine light on the less clear passages in the Bible. In this case you don't have to look very far for clearer verses, as John begins his gospel by explaining that Jesus isn't a created being, but the Word who created all things (John 1:1,10). So *begotten* must mean something really unique about the incarnation of Jesus.

Three Persons

There was another guy, a third-century priest named Sabellius, who had sketchy beliefs and got God wrong too. Unlike Arius, he didn't believe Jesus was a created being, but he argued that Jesus was fully God in a sketchy kind of way. His teaching denied what Christians believe about the Trinity.

Sabellius used the analogy of the sun to explain God. With the sun, you have three things. You have the star, the sun. You have the light that comes from the sun. Finally, you have the heat emanating from the sun. You can see why some might think this would prove to be a useful way to explain the Trinity. It's three things in one, right? Not really.

You may have noticed in this analogy, while the light and heat come from the sun, they are not the sun. They exist apart from the sun. If Jesus and the Spirit are just emanating from God like the light and heat emanate from the sun, then you don't have a biblical depiction of God. You have something other than the Trinity. That sounds like a sketchy view of God.

This sketchy view is known as *modalism*. In defending the belief in one God, those who believe in modalism teach that when the Bible mentions the Father, or the Son, or the Spirit, it doesn't mean three distinct persons. Instead, modalism argues these are all different manifestations of God. These manifestations are not individual persons.

Think about this like video games where you can choose a different avatar or skin. You can be a superhero. You can be a barnyard animal. You can be your favorite cartoon. You can be a banana with legs and arms and a face. You can choose whatever skin you want to play your game. Each avatar represents you, but none of them are you. They are just different manifestations of you in the game.

Is this how we should understand God? Does God just choose different avatars in different places? In some places he is God the Father, in some places he is the Son, and in other places the Spirit? Is that a good way to make sense of God or is it a little sketchy? Are the places God shows up in Scripture just avatars for the one God? When you read the Bible, does it seem like the Son is just an avatar? Is the Spirit just an avatar? What do you do when you get all three persons of the Trinity interacting with one another?

In creation we see God and also God's Spirit (Genesis 1:1–2). In Jesus's baptism, we see all three, God the Father, God the Son, and God the Spirit (Mark 1:9–12). Jesus commands us to baptize believers in the name of all three: the Father, Son, and Spirit (Matthew 28:19). Is the avatar analogy the best way to make sense of this? How do these different manifestations of the one God all show up at the same time and interact with each other? If they are just avatars like a video game, how is it that they all show up at the same time?

In contrast, the doctrine of the Trinity makes sense of these passages. That's not to say the Trinity makes perfect sense. It's a mystery. But it does make sense of the biblical data. That's pretty important for our theology, isn't it?

The doctrine of the Trinity lines up with the way we see God the Father in the Bible. As God told Isaiah: ". . . so that all may know from the rising of the sun to its setting that there is no one but me. I am the LORD, and there is no other" (Isaiah 45:6). It's clear there is only one God. Jesus taught us to pray to God as our heavenly Father (Matthew 6:9).

When you read the word *God* in the Bible, it's generally speaking of God the Father. Does that mean the Son and the Spirit are something less than God or merely manifestations of him? Absolutely not. We have to let all of Scripture form our view. We have to let the clearer bits help us understand the less clear.

As we've already touched on, the New Testament clearly presents Jesus as God. Just because Jesus prays to God the Father doesn't mean Jesus is less than God himself. Again, how do you make sense of this without the Trinity? You can't. The Trinity is the key.

From Jesus's actions and teachings, we see clear evidence of his claim to be divine. As Paul says, it was because of his love that he humbled himself to endure God's wrath for our sin (Philippians 2:1–11). One day every knee will bow and recognize his true authority. Jesus is a person. Jesus is God. That doesn't make sense without the Trinity.

What about the Spirit? We might think of him as an impersonal, misty, ghostlike character. After all, Jesus says he's like the wind (John 3:8). Was Jesus teaching us God the Spirit is an impersonal force like the wind? Not at all. In that particular context, Jesus was showing how humans can't control the Spirit.

Throughout the Bible we see the Holy Spirit's active work in the world. He empowers God's prophets (Isaiah 48:16). Like a person, he can be grieved (Ephesians 4:30) or lied to (Acts 5:4). He searches the things of God the Father (1 Corinthians 2:10). The Spirit helps us and intercedes for us (Romans 8:26–27). Sounds like a person to me.

To go back to your kidnapping scenario, if you read through the Bible and followed the data, I believe it would lead you to something like the doctrine of the Trinity. God is one. God exists as three persons. Each person is fully God. It's a mystery, but it's a mystery within biblical boundaries. The stream of orthodoxy is flowing between these two points, these two banks—the oneness of God on the one side and the doctrine of the Trinity on the other.

The Human Data

The Trinity makes sense of more things than just the biblical data. As I mentioned in the beginning of the book, I'll often get philosophical on stuff like this. The Bible is the most important starting point, but does what we believe from the Bible help us make sense of the world we live in? I think so.

By understanding more about God we can make better sense of the human condition. Earlier we considered the "cosmological argument": if the material universe had a beginning, what might its cause be? From that argument we concluded the cause of the universe must be outside of time, space, matter, and energy. But there's more.

If the universe had a beginning at some point in the past, it stands to reason the source of creation is personal because this source or cause was able to choose to create the universe. If the source of the universe was not personal, then why isn't the universe eternal? Maybe an illustration will help.[1]

If there was a baseball, one that existed forever, it wouldn't need some kind of explanation. It's just always been. We can call it the "eternal baseball." But for baseballs that began to exist, those baseballs that were created, someone at some point in time chose to create them. The fact that they have a beginning at some point in the past shows us someone came along and crafted the leather and stitches and put together whatever else goes into a baseball.

The same is true of the universe, which you can think about as a very large baseball. If the universe began to exist, not only must its cause be outside of time, space, matter, and energy, as we've discussed, but its cause must also be able to choose to create a universe. Agency, the ability to choose and act, is a property of personhood. The fact the universe had a beginning points to a personal source.

Some might object by saying the universe could be an accident caused by material stuff that existed before the universe came into being. On one level, that might seem persuasive. But it just pushes the argument back further. The problem is still there, even if it takes a bit longer to get to it. For example, where did the stuff that existed before the big bang come from? You still have some explaining to do if you choose to go that path.

If we buy into a view of reality that some impersonal and irrational matter is responsible for everything, that it somehow created the world by accident, then we might get a momentary explanation for the world without God. But here's the trade-off. We will lose the very foundation of what it means to be human.

This is an argument C. S. Lewis loved to use.[2] If the world is ultimately an accident, then so are you. If you are an accident, then so is your brain. If your brain is an accident, then so are your thoughts. If your thoughts are accidents, then why do you trust them? Without a personal and intelligent source behind the world, we end up losing the ability to trust our own minds.

Furthermore, if the universe is really traced back to some impersonal source, then why do we seem to be persons with the ability to choose and act? Where does that come from? We are able to choose, to love, and to give of ourselves to others. If we are personal, then it makes sense that the cause of our whole world is personal as well.

While it's a mystery beyond our ability to fully understand, it's a mystery that kind of makes sense of our predicament as personal beings living in a confusing world. The world is filled with relationships: love, friendship, affection, and care. It all points back to a time before our world was spoken into existence, where there existed an eternal community—the Trinity, who chose to create a world populated with persons made in the image of God.

Even our scrolling on social media reminds us we don't come from some impersonal, primordial soup. Our longing for belonging points to a God who invites us to share in his joy flowing from the eternal community of the Trinity. This is the very thing for which we were created. God who has eternally existed as a perfect community within himself, fully satisfied, in need of nothing, invites us into this fellowship. That's pretty amazing, if you ask me.

The opportunity to know, love, and worship God is an invitation into the joy-filled community of the God who is Father, Son, and Spirit. What a picture of eternal life! Our desire for relationships, connection, and community is pointing beyond ourselves, isn't it? Every relationship at some point disappoints, yet still we long for full acceptance and belonging. These longings point to God.

The Philosophical Data

Throughout human history people have wondered about how to make sense of it all. I mean, you look around and there's just a whole lot going on, isn't there? You've got sky. You've got water. You've got land. You've got fire. There's a bunch of stuff in the world. Then there's also us. And there's a ton of diversity among all the creatures, from mice to men. How do we make sense of all that?[3]

Centuries ago, a Greek philosopher named Thales of Miletus thought he had it all figured out. In looking for a way to make sense of all the diversity, he thought water was a good candidate. Maybe H_2O could be the one thing that unifies everything else. After all, it can be a solid, a gas, or a liquid. Everything seems to fit into those buckets, if you will. Also, if you look at the ocean tides, it seems like water possesses the ability to move itself. Water seemed to provide a good candidate for ultimate reality.

Not everyone was convinced. Some other philosophers thought Thales was all wet. Pythagoras, known for his math theories, loved fire. He believed fire was the one thing that was really real. Everything else could be understood in light of this powerful force.

Still another philosopher came along and said ultimate reality was really four things: water, fire, air, and earth. That's the origin of the comic heroes the Fantastic Four. All this illustrates the problem: these philosophers, at best, reduced everything down to four fundamental explanations. But the original question was—what is the one thing that allows us to make sense of everything else?

So philosophers continued their search. They sought a fifth essence to make sense of the other stuff. They wanted to find the one thing that made sense of all the other things. The fifth essence was called the "quintessence." We still use that term today when we describe someone as the ideal leader or communicator and call them "quintessential."

Fast forward from ancient Greece to our day, and you'll see that people are still trying to find a unity for all the diversity. That's where our term *university* comes from, a compound of the words *unity* and *diversity*.

Even modern scientists look for a single theory to understand all reality. Some call it a G.U.T., a grand unifying theory. Others call it a T.O.E., a theory of everything. Either way, they're wondering the same thing: what is a simple way to make sense of the complexities of the cosmos? How is it possible to have a perfect unity in the midst of the diversity?

The doctrine of the Trinity. There is one God who exists eternally as three persons. Each person is fully God. And he is the author and sustainer of all things. To go back to the earlier Lewis quote, he doctrine of the Trinity functions like the rising sun. It shines light on the world, helping us to make sense of things. It's the key that unlocks the mystery of reality.

Questions for Reflection

1. What analogy have you heard about the Trinity that you found helpful?
2. What are some ways that analogy is limited, and if taken too far, can lead to a sketchy view of God?
3. Which discussion about the Trinity in this chapter did you find helpful? Explain why.
4. How might you explain the doctrine of the Trinity to a new believer who is still trying to figure it out?
5. Can we fully understand the Trinity? Why or why not?

The Ocean in a Teacup

We, who have God and conscience on our side,
have a majority against the universe.
—FREDERICK DOUGLASS

A friend once described theology as trying to fit the ocean into a teacup. I like that. While we can't fit the ocean into a teacup, we can fit ourselves into the ocean. In the same way, our theology can't fully capture God. But our theology can and should be big enough to capture us.

It's sad that some reduce God to something they can manage, control, and fully comprehend. Don't settle for a *mini theology*, a sketchy view, forcing your beliefs of God into a shape that no longer fits the Bible. Again, to go back to our method of doing theology in the first chapter, we have to let the mysteries of the Bible speak for themselves and not try muzzle them to make ourselves more comfortable. If you could make perfect sense of God, he wouldn't be that impressive, would he? If you could understand God, you would, well, probably be God. That would be the sketchiest view of all, wouldn't it?

As we've said along our river journey, if we stay within both banks, it's possible to avoid sketchy views while we form true beliefs about God. While we can't comprehend everything about God, we can form true beliefs about him. You can think about what we've covered so far about the doctrine of God as a funnel. We started big picture then worked our way down to narrower principles.

We began with a God who exists, who is personal, and who has revealed himself in Scripture (chapters 2–4). Then we considered how the triune God is independent of time, space, matter, and energy (chapters 4–6). As the author and apologist William Lane Craig likes to say, "God is the source and sustainer of all reality that exists outside himself."[1]

Framing the Argument

In braving the rapids of orthodoxy, we've seen how God is a mystery too great for words. Yet he is a mystery revealed within boundaries, the contours of which we can trace in the Bible. The orthodox view of God flows through the banks of Scripture.

We can allow these truths to frame our view of God and keep us from wrong views. And even though people have run aground on one bank or the other, we should allow the tension between God as one and God as Trinity to form how we think about him. Yet our aim isn't only to avoid sketchy views.

Our theology is more like standing on a bridge with a sense of awe about the current as its waves crash beneath us. This isn't a burden we have to bear; it's a wonder we get to behold. Yes, there are boundaries, but they are more like a frame showcasing a beautiful painting—one that we adore but can't fully control. In the previous chapter, we looked at the picture frame, that God is both one and also a Trinity. In this chapter, we aim to study the painting itself. Who exactly is God? How do you answer this ocean-in-a-teacup question?

There's a solution to this God-sized problem. It's surprisingly simple. Throughout the history of the Christian church, leading thinkers have sought to keep believers from sketchy views of the triune God with a doctrine called *Divine Simplicity*. Theologians debate over how to best define and apply this doctrine, but I've found it to be a helpful tool in thinking about all that we see about God in the Bible.

I once heard a funny illustration about our attempt to make God something less than who he is: "God is either God or he is not, in the same way a pregnant woman cannot be *kind of* pregnant." There is no "kind of God" in the same way as there is no "kind of pregnant." It's an all or nothing situation.

God is God. We never see half God, or kind of God, or little God versus big God, or angry God versus happy God. God is always God. He is one, and he never changes. We can accept him or reject him, but we cannot compartmentalize or redefine him. All that we see about God in Scripture is true of God.

What if God Was Like Us?

In the following paragraphs I'll outline some implications of this as it relates to our goal of keeping our thoughts about God well centered in the stream of orthodoxy. We'll look at how God does not have *parts*, *passions*, or *potential*. Before we get there, we need to carefully consider the sorts of ways the Bible talks about God, that if misunderstood, can get us off track.

Earlier we looked at the illustration of a black and white television set. Even if hooked up to a device to play a full-color movie, the picture would just come out in shades of gray. No matter how vibrant the content you're broadcasting to the screen might be, the television has limitations on what it can display.

Again, this is the kind of situation we are in with God. As amazing as he is, we don't have categories to fully make sense of him. After all, he's in a category of his own. That's why God communicates to us using language we can understand, for our benefit, even though such language can surely never fully capture all of who he is.

If God is to communicate to us in ways we can understand, he's going to have to condescend to us, to stoop down to our level, and use human language and terms. And since the inspired biblical authors are humans themselves, they are going to use language familiar to them and their original audience. This is simply how communication works.

Figurative language

We should always take the Bible seriously, even when we recognize parts that are not intended to be understood literally. For example, when the psalmist says the "mountains skipped like lambs" in Psalm 114:4, no one reads that to mean the landscape was moving around in some whimsical kind of way, bouncing up and down, on the particular day the psalm was written. It's poetic language.

We receive the Bible as it was given to us. If an author uses an expression in a nonliteral way, we need to seek to understand that and respond accordingly. We can often figure this out by looking at how different forms or expressions are used elsewhere in the Bible. For the most part, this is pretty straightforward as we read the Bible.

For example, in Genesis 5, Moses says Enoch "walked with God." Here it doesn't mention a garden like in the opening chapters of Genesis. It merely says Enoch walked with God, and God took him (Genesis 5:21–24). The focus is on relationship, on spiritual intimacy between God and Enoch.

Since the apostle John says no one has ever seen God, we know this talk of God walking with people isn't to be read literally but instead relationally (John 1:18). Enoch wasn't looking over at God as they walked along. God had an intimate relationship, a friendship, with Enoch.

We can be God's friends too. We sometimes use this same kind of language, don't we? We might talk about someone we consider to be a faithful Christian and refer to their "walk with God." When we do that, we're using human terms to point to a greater reality.

Anthropomorphic language

Sometimes the Bible describes God in human terms too. This kind of language is called *anthropomorphic*. This big word means "man" and "form." We see this kind of language when God is talked about in human forms. God isn't a human, but he's communicating with humans, so he does so in ways they understand. His language is an expression of love.

To revisit the walking example, we know what it means to "walk." Unless we've suffered from a birth defect or tragic accident, we're able to use our legs and feet. So when Moses says God "walked" in the garden of Eden, should we think that God had feet like we do? Does God have legs? No. We should see that Moses is communicating to us in a way we can understand using *anthropomorphic* language.

When Isaiah describes that God's "ear" is not deaf that he cannot hear, and his "arm" is not so short that he cannot save, is he really implying God has ears and arms (Isaiah 59:1)? Of course not. We have biblical passages making it clear God is spirit and not something material (John 4:24). Thus, we interpret these *anthropomorphic* passages as pointing to a deeper reality by using language humans can relate to.

Anthropomorphic language is common in Scripture. So much so, the theologian Herman Bavinck said the Bible is anthropomorphic "through and through."[2] That means we have to be careful and cautious in making sense of the language about God that sounds really human. We must understand passages containing anthropomorphic language, considering what we know to be true about God.

Incarnational reality

Now all this changes with Jesus. The scandal of the incarnation is that the second person of the Trinity, the Son, took on human nature, flesh, and literally walked among us. This is clear in the text. We're not wondering if the apostles really meant Jesus was a real person or if they were using anthropomorphic language. It's clear they were being literal. But that's very different from the Old Testament references to God.

One thing to keep in mind, particularly with the Old Testament passages, is the difference between something that is *descriptive* versus something that is *prescriptive*. For example, it's one thing if I described how someone took a particular pill and got better. I'm describing what they did—*descriptive*. That's not the same thing their doctor did for them though. Their doctor prescribed the pill for them—*prescriptive*. That's why we call it a prescription.

Just because I described how a pill helped them, I'm not prescribing for you to take the same pill. That would be an example of confusing description with prescription. In a similar way, if an Old Testament passage *describes* something like God having ears, legs, or hands, that is altogether different than other passages that clearly *prescribe* what we are to believe about God. The distinction between description and prescription can be a handy tool when studying the Bible.

Prescriptive. If you know the Ten Commandments in Exodus, you likely remember that in the second commandment God clearly told his people not to make images or idols depicting him. And yet some Old Testament passages describe God in human terms, giving us a mental image of God walking. Are such passages violating the second commandment? No.

In such cases, the authors aren't trying to get us to think of God in material ways. They are communicating truths about God using anthropomorphic language so that we can better understand. Their goal is not for us to think God stands six foot two and walks on legs and feet.

Descriptive. There are plenty of passages that clearly prescribe what to believe about God: that he is one, that he is a spirit, that he exists as Father, Son, and Spirit, etc. We view the descriptive passages in the Old Testament through the lens of the prescriptive passages that teach us what to think about God. If we take the descriptive passages too literally, we will not only miss the point, we will move away from the main current in the stream of orthodoxy.

We have to let the prescriptive passages, the clearer teachings about what we are to believe, inform how we make sense of the descriptive passages. We have to let what we can understand illuminate the parts we may find more difficult to understand.

God without Parts

Speaking of language I can understand, let's talk about pizza. In the epic battle between deep dish Chicago style and the New York thin crust, who's right? When I'm hungry, I don't really care. I'll eat and enjoy them both. But to be totally honest, even though I'm from the state of Illinois, and I love that mile-high pie you have to eat with a fork, I tend to prefer a thin slice I can fold in half. Don't judge. I still love my home state.

What's this have to do with God? Sometimes, people can be tempted to think of God like a pizza. We might assume God has different parts, or in this case, slices, some of which are more godlike than others. If we were to think of God as a pizza, we might assume one slice is way bigger than the other. Maybe the God the Father slice is the biggest, the Jesus slice is the second biggest, and the Spirit slice is a mere sliver.

Or perhaps you could think about the pizza as being divided into two halves, like the Old and New Testaments. The two slices could be equal in size, one representing God the Father and the other God the Son. The Spirit could be the sauce that both halves share in common. While that might be a good meal, it wouldn't be a good analogy. Yet when we think of God as three persons, it's hard to avoid some mental concept of God as divided in some way between the three. We must respect the biblical boundaries around the mystery of God and attempt to say what the Bible says and not confuse it, add to it, or take away from it. While theology can be complicated, we don't want to overcomplicate God in our attempt to understand him.

To carry the pizza metaphor much further than necessary, another sketchy way to think about God is as if each person of the Trinity (or slice in the case of the pizza) has unique qualities in comparison to the others. It would be like a thin-crust pizza cut into three slices, where one slice has spicy pepperoni, another has anchovies, and the last slice has vegetables. Sure, the whole thing is one pizza, but each slice is different from the others in significant ways. Is that a good way to understand God?

It would be wrong to think of the Trinity as divided into parts, like a pizza cut three ways. Furthermore, it would be wrong to think the persons of the Trinity have separate qualities like a pizza with one-third toppings. But just how should you think about the Trinity then? Before I answer that, I think I need to step out and get some pizza. I'm a bit hangry at the moment. Be right back.

As I hope you've seen, the pizza metaphor implies God has parts. But, as we've discussed, God is omnipresent, existing without spatial features or limitations, outside of time and space. To think of God like a three-piece pizza would require each person of the Trinity to have different properties than the other persons of the Trinity. How could that be if God doesn't have spatial features or limitations? If God doesn't have features, then he can't be divided into different parts. God is one.

It can all get rather confusing. Theology can hurt your brain at times. I get it. G. K. Chesterton is often quoted as saying, "Theology is that part of religion that requires brains."[3] He was right.

Your brain is required to do theology but that doesn't mean your brain is entirely up to the job. Yet you are capable of seeing the biblical boundaries around the doctrine of God. Again, you can truly know things without understanding them fully. It's like seeing the tip of an iceberg. You understand there's a lot more beneath the surface even though you can't see it all.

With God, it's far different than the iceberg scenario. With an iceberg we can find ways to go beneath the surface. It might be inconvenient and quite cold, but we could find a way. With God, we must content ourselves with what he's revealed about himself. In other words, there are things beneath the surface, and we don't have a way to get down there.

Historically, Christian leaders have navigated these biblical boundaries by sticking to a *simple* understanding of God's essence. The theologian Gerald Bray describes the doctrine of simplicity as the most "fundamental attribute of God's being."[4] Bray explains that whatever we say about God, since God is one, applies to the "totality of his being."[5]

This doctrine works well with how we're trying to let the clearer parts of Scripture shed light on the less clear parts. For example, if God "is one" (Deuteronomy 6:4), then whatever else we say about God must flow out of his being, which doesn't change. There's a lot we can and must say about God, but it needs to be understood within the reality that God is one.

Throughout church history theologians have tried to make sense of the God of the Bible. In the fourth century, a church leader named Augustine described God as "simple and indivisible." In the early twelfth century Anslem said God is "in no wise composite, but is supremely simple, supremely immutable [i.e., unchanging]." In the thirteenth century Thomas Aquinas said, "It is clear that God is in no way composite, but is altogether simple."[6]

Since it's straightforward in the Bible there is only one God, we need to use that as a framework for making sense of everything else that's said about God. That's not always easy. It can be difficult to think of God as three persons without somehow thinking about him as having different properties or parts, like the mouthwatering pizza example. The fact that God "is one" can keep us within the banks of Scripture and away from sketchy views.

There have been some who took the teachings about God as Father, Son, and Spirit to mean there are three gods, a view called *tritheism*. Others have thought each person of the trinity was only partially God, a view known as *partialism*. We need to keep our eye on the oneness of God to avoid such sketchy views.

Keeping the oneness of God in mind will protect us from the sketchy view that sees the different persons of the Trinity as somehow less than God. If God is one and indivisible, it makes perfect sense when Jesus says that he and the Father are one, and that if anyone has seen him, they have seen the Father (John 14:9). Jesus is fully God. If you see him, you've seen the Father.

If we try to make sense of the Trinity without keeping our eye on the oneness of God, we could easily begin saying sketchy things about the persons of the Trinity that don't fit the Bible well. That's why Christians over the years have been very careful in how they word their beliefs about God. They strived to make their beliefs about the Trinity clear because they saw the danger of viewing Jesus as being a little less than God, or even worse, as a created being.

Check out this summary called The Nicene Creed from the third century:

We believe in one God,
the Father almighty,
maker of heaven and earth,
of all things visible and invisible.

And in one Lord Jesus Christ,
the only Son of God,
begotten from the Father before all ages,
God from God,
Light from Light,
true God from true God,
begotten, not made;
of the same essence as the Father.
Through him all things were made.
For us and for our salvation
he came down from heaven;
he became incarnate by the Holy Spirit and the virgin Mary,
and was made human.
He was crucified for us under Pontius Pilate;
he suffered and was buried.
The third day he rose again, according to the Scriptures.
He ascended to heaven
and is seated at the right hand of the Father.

He will come again with glory
to judge the living and the dead.
His kingdom will never end.

And we believe in the Holy Spirit,
the Lord, the giver of life.
He proceeds from the Father and the Son,
and with the Father and the Son is worshiped and
glorified.
He spoke through the prophets.
We believe in one holy catholic [i.e., universal] and
apostolic church.
We affirm one baptism for the forgiveness of sins.
We look forward to the resurrection of the dead,
and to life in the world to come. Amen.

While you might not immediately understand the reasoning behind every line in this creed, you can see how it tries to make crystal clear the belief that Jesus is God. He is of the same essence as the Father. The creed is also framing the way we should think about Jesus—as begotten, like in John 3:16, where Jesus is described as "God's only begotten Son" (KJV).

So a creed like this illustrates once again how the Bible establishes the boundaries—like banks of a river—within which we form an orthodox view of God. This doesn't mean we remove the mystery of God in the Bible. That's something we can't do. God is God—in full color—even if we're just seeing him through our black and white televisions.

God exists eternally as Father, Son, and Spirit. We can't and shouldn't want to change that. This our very source of comfort in life and death.

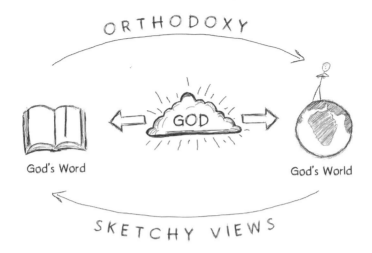

God without Passions

Have you ever seen someone so moved by emotion that you could tell their brain had kind of checked out? Maybe you've been there yourself. Sadly, I know I have. Whether it's the result of anger, frustration, confusion, or despair, there's a certain look in a person's eyes when they're operating on pure emotion. God never experiences this.

Impossible passions

The *doctrine of impassibility* describes how God isn't controlled by passions. While I hope you have control over your emotions, at least most of the time, you can certainly relate to experiencing emotions that don't match reality. Think of a surprise birthday party. You walk into a dark room, and all of a sudden, a lot of people jump out at you. Your immediate response might be shock or fear, but in your rational mind you'd be elated or happy. God never experiences anything like this.

There's never a time when God's emotions dictate his attitude toward a situation. God is never out of control.

Now, to be clear, there are plenty of passages in the Bible that talk about God having feelings. Again, this is anthropomorphic language. Passions or emotions don't affect God the way emotions affect us. We can't read our experience into God.

So whatever it means in such *descriptive* passages about God, we must keep the *prescriptive* passages in mind. For example, Malachi 3:6 that tells us God never changes, and Hebrews 13:8 says Jesus is the same yesterday, today, and forever. When we see a change in God's mood, we need to ask how this change fits with passages that say God doesn't change. How can we make sense of the two realities—passages that say God doesn't change and passages that describe God changing from anger to delight.

Here's the way I try to help my students think about this topic. God has a fixed attitude toward every possible situation. For example, God feels a certain way toward sin. He always has. He always will. God feels a certain way toward repentance. He always has. He always will.

So if, in a given passage, we see God angry at sin, it has nothing to do with God changing. That's who God is. If we see God pleased by repentance, this has nothing to do with God changing. That's who God is.

In such cases, what has changed isn't God. The situation has changed. God has a fixed attitude toward every situation, and if the situation changes, we will see God's fixed attitude toward that changed situation. The clear passages in Scripture teaching us God doesn't change, *prescriptive* passages, help us make sense of less clear passages where it seems like God is changing, *descriptive* passages.

Impossible solutions

I remember as a kid getting irritated at the Rubik's Cube. I couldn't figure the dumb thing out. Unlike my kids today, I couldn't watch YouTube videos to learn the patterns for solving the multicolored, three-dimensional puzzle from the underworld. The more I turned that square, the more the colors got jumbled. If you've learned how to work a Rubik's Cube, you know there are some set patterns to follow to get all the colors lined up. If you don't know the patterns, it always feels a bit arbitrary, or willy-nilly, as if the thing just refuses to comply.

So I did what any young kid would do who wanted to get it right but just couldn't. I peeled the stickers off and then put them back on with all the colors on the right sides. To be honest, it wasn't very convincing. In peeling them off they lost a lot of their stickiness; now the color squares were just barely hanging off their spots. I didn't fool anybody.

I hadn't solved the puzzle. I had only changed the properties of the Rubik's Cube to fit my purposes. Sometimes we think we can do this with God. We think we can manipulate him so that his emotion will lead him to do something contrary to what we know to be true of his character. Unlike the Rubik's Cube, this is impossible. We can't get God to make an emotional decision.

God's actions are always perfectly proportionate to his character. God's character never changes. When it looks like God has changed in the Bible, we should explore those passages for changes in the situation: people's attitudes, behaviors, and decisions—not changes with God's character or being.

Look at how James describes God, "Every good and perfect gift is from above, coming down from the Father of lights, who does not change like shifting shadows" (James 1:17). There is not even a shadow of turning with God. When we see an emotion of God in the Bible, we can stop and think, "Hmmm . . . that must be God's fixed attitude toward that situation."

This is true of examples where it looks like God is changing his mind in the Bible. Think about the salty story of Sodom and Gomorrah. God was going to nuke the whole place. Abraham stands up and intercedes, pleading that if there were only fifty—nay even only ten—righteous persons, for God not to destroy them. You can read about it in Genesis 18.

Sometimes people will point to this as proof that God changed his mind. Though God held off his judgment for a short time, he still destroyed them in the end. Lot barely made it out. His wife didn't. Even if we grant that God temporarily withheld his judgment as a result of Abraham's prayer, God still did what he said he would do in the first place in Genesis 19.

This shows us God has a fixed attitude toward the prayers of the righteous. Did God know what would happen with these people? We'll talk more about this in a moment, but for now let me just say yes, he did.

When Abraham intercedes, and the messengers are able to convince Lot to leave the city, we should see this as a result of God's fixed attitude toward the prayers of the righteous man Abraham, not the result of a change in God. Again, consider the prescriptive explanation from James, "The prayer of a righteous person is very powerful in its effect" (James 5:16). God has a fixed attitude toward the prayers of the righteous. This is what changed in the scenario; it wasn't a change in God's character.

A God with No Potential?

Has it ever bothered you when someone tells you have potential? It means they see something in you that's still underdeveloped. They see what you could be. But it can sometimes bother us, because we'd rather hear about how far we have come, not how far we have yet to go. When someone tells you they see potential in you, they are encouraging you, that in time you can become even better. They see signs of your future greatness now. My point here is that this talk of future potential never applies to God.

Here's why. God is who he is. He isn't going to become more God or less God. There's no God 2.0 as compared to God 1.0. While there have been sketchy views in the history of the church that line up with this kind of thinking, they do not line up with the Bible. They are sketchy views of God.

No potential for changing

Let's consider the heretic Marcion again. As I pointed out, he was born around the time the apostle John was writing his gospel and the book of Revelation. This shows it didn't take long for people to try to steer Christianity in a sketchy way. Marcion didn't like the God of the Old Testament. Instead, he saw Jesus as a far better spokesperson. He thought the Scripture should reflect this.

In review, Marcion did this by rejecting all the Old Testament and most of the New Testament. His overarching concern was to highlight the loving Christ of Christianity versus the angry Old Testament deity worshiped earlier by the Jews. He wanted a god who had evolved from the Old Testament to the New, a god who better fit his experiences and expectations. But again, creating any god from our own wishful thinking is rightly condemned as idolatry. The Bible should govern how we view our experiences and expectations, not the other way around.

It took me a long time to understand and embrace the doctrine of *impassibility*. After all, on the one hand, I've always understood on some level God's emotions don't fluctuate, although some verses in the Bible communicate that God does seem to experience emotions. On the other hand, I accept the Christian doctrine of *immutability*, that God himself never changes, because it seems clear in Scripture, that "God is not a man, that he might lie, or a son of man, that he might change his mind (Numbers 23:19).

We must let the clear passages that *prescribe* that God doesn't change make sense of the passages that *describe* God as changing. God isn't controlled by passions, and he doesn't have potential. He is who he is, and he never changes. He never acts in a way that is inconsistent with his character. Let's consider the Bible's biggest fish story. I told you there would be more fishing references in this book, didn't I?

Think about Jonah and Nineveh. God's message through Jonah was that Nineveh would be destroyed in forty days (Jonah 3:4). But then God doesn't judge them, a fact Jonah was not too happy about. What's going on there? Did God change his mind? We can find the answer in the next verse, "Then the people of Nineveh believed God. . ." (Jonah 3:5).

God's message of judgment was consistent with God's fixed attitude toward evil. God's forgiveness of them is based on God's fixed attitude toward repentance. The people of Nineveh repented. They saw a different side of God, namely God's fixed attitude toward their seeking him.

In passages like this, it's not that God's essence has taken on new properties or lost old ones. Again, God doesn't have potential. He's not becoming nicer or meaner. He's not getting better with working with people. It's not that God is so moved by love that he overlooks evil. What has changed is the human scenario. When the situation changes, we see a different attitude of God that is fixed in his eternal character.

We must keep in mind the Bible's use of *anthropomorphic* language to describe God and his actions. This will keep us between the banks of the stream of orthodoxy, so we don't develop sketchy views as we navigate our way through the Bible.

No potential for learning

Think about the following questions: Does God know everything? Did God know what would happen in Nineveh after Jonah preached to them? Of course. Was God surprised in any way? Of course not.

So why would God present the scenario as conditional? Why tell them he would judge them, when in the end he didn't judge them? Did God change? No. They changed. The situation changed, and the people of Nineveh then saw God's fixed attitude toward repentance, which is always forgiveness. But the whole episode took place in history, in time and space, with one event following another. So that's exactly how it's recorded for us, even though God knows "the end from the beginning" (Isaiah 46:10).

Again, when you read the story of Jonah, keep this in mind: what changed in this scenario? It wasn't God who changed. This reminds me of a preacher's illustration I heard years ago about a married couple who always sat close to each other on the bench seat in their old truck. That made it possible for his wife to slide over from the passenger seat and sit in the middle, close to her husband.

When the couple were first married, the wife would always sit in this middle seat as close to her husband as possible. He would drive with one hand on the steering wheel and one arm around her. Over the years she drifted over toward the passenger seat. One day she remarked, as they drove down the road, "It feels like we're not as close as we used to be." The husband quickly responded, "I'm not the one who moved." Indeed, he was still sitting precisely where he always had behind the steering wheel.

God is predictable like this. He hasn't moved. He hasn't changed. He never has. He never will.

We humans, on the other hand, often allow our passions and misunderstandings, and our limited amount of knowledge of a situation, to lead us to do things we otherwise wouldn't do. We get mad, and we bang our hand down on the table or stomp our foot. If everything was going well, and we were otherwise perfectly happy, we wouldn't all of a sudden hit the table or slam our foot down, would we? Why might we do it when we're mad? It's because our passions are taking over. In such cases, our actions don't line up with our reason.

God never experiences this. His perfect actions are always aligned with his perfect understanding. God never changes his fixed attitudes. If situations change, we will see God's fixed attitude toward the changed situation. Again, God isn't the one changing. God isn't learning new facts. Nonetheless, the Bible describes events in terms humans can understand.

If God were ever to learn a new fact, that would mean he isn't *omniscient*, the reality that God possesses all knowledge. His knowledge, before he learned the new fact, would somehow be less than afterward. So, as I write this, if God doesn't know the future, then he's learning what I'm about to type as I type it.

If this sketchy view were true, it would mean all our actions add to God's knowledge. And that means if God has potential to learn new things, like what I would or wouldn't do in the future, then once I've done the thing, I've contributed to God's knowledge. But would these kinds of conclusions line up with Scripture?

No potential for limitations

If God knows all our future decisions, does that mean they are entirely predetermined, and we are not responsible? In reading the Bible it certainly seems like people make real decisions. It seems like Adam and Eve make true decisions when they choose to eat from the Tree of Knowledge of Good and Evil. It appears Pharaoh makes a choice not to let Moses and the Israelites leave Egypt, then later makes the choice to let them go, only to then make the choice to chase after them.

Yet at the same time, the Bible teaches that God is in control of everything, including the hearts of men. King Solomon wrote that the "king's heart is like channeled water in the Lord's hand: [God] directs it wherever he chooses" (Proverbs 21:1). There's nothing outside his control. If God's control of everything is unlimited, then how can people make real choices?

All this gets into what I describe to my students as the mysterious way the Creator acts with his creation. It's easy to try to make sense of why a person might react in a particular way toward the actions of another person, but does this really give us categories for explaining how God works with us? As we've said, God is in a category of his own. That surely means the way God acts with his creation will include certain things beyond the scope of human reason.

A philosopher friend of mine helped me once as we talked about this topic. He said just because there isn't a human category for how God can be in control of everything, and humans still make real decisions, doesn't mean it's impossible for God to create a world in which people are free and God is still in control. This would certainly not be impossible for God. It might be difficult, or even impossible, for me to make sense of, but that certainly doesn't make it impossible for God. While my understanding is limited, he is without limits.

There are a lot of ways to try to account for this tension. Some systems alter one side of the equation or the other to make it more understandable. Whether we lean into man's freedom, or into God's divine plan, I think we all hit certain limits. Even the systems I find compelling only take us so far. The Bible presents both as true: God is sovereign. Humanity is somehow free to choose and thus accountable. It's a paradox. It's the two sides of the stream of orthodoxy.

Even here there are real limitations in the words we use to talk about this reality. What is a choice if the person making it has, well, no choice? Are we merely responsible for the consequences of our choices but not really able to make true choices? These are things theologians and philosophers like to argue about. I get it. But like with other things, I believe this is a mystery within certain boundaries.

We can't deny the clear teachings of the Bible simply to feel better about our experience. Our theories serve the Bible, not the other way around. There are things in the Bible that don't always fit our preconceived notions, expectations, or even neatly designed systems. I'm reminded again of the words of Moses, "The hidden things belong to the LORD our God, but the revealed things [i.e., the Scriptures] belong to us and our children forever, so that we may follow all the words of this law" (Deuteronomy 29:29).

We can spend our whole lives investigating every system of thought. We can wrap our minds around theories with big terms like Arminianism, Calvinism, and Molinism and still have questions about how to make them fit with what's going on in the Bible. If you're unfamiliar with those terms, they are different ways of trying to make sense of God's sovereignty over his creation.

You may already have a clear system you prefer, like one mentioned above. My point is simply this—no system can remove all the mystery. We must resist the equal temptations to ignore the tension or to force a resolution. I don't want to imply all systems of theology related to this topic are equal. Surely, some must be closer to reality than others.

But I'd like to humbly suggest that no system can fully capture how God relates to his creation and vice versa.

When all the facts are known and properly understood—there will be no real conflict. But if we're not careful, we will end up embracing one sketchy view or another in our attempt to avoid paradox. Some theologians go so far as to suggest that God doesn't know the future as one way of dealing with this topic. This serves as a reminder we can't violate clear teaching in Scripture to resolve what seems to be, well, beyond resolution. Instead, live between the banks of paradox.

God knows everything. He is sovereign. The apostles pleaded with people to repent and believe, so the Bible depicts humans as making real decisions. Don't try to water down God's sovereignty or dilute human agency to make your theology more comfortable or manageable. Don't be sketchy like that.

For Our Good

To be honest, there should be a lot of comfort for the Christian in considering these truths. **First, if God is one, meaning one essence, and isn't in any way divided, then God is whole.** There's not some wild inconsistency in God. This is what is meant by God is without part or passion. God isn't fluctuating between one part of himself and another. Whenever we see God's holiness, we are also seeing his love. God is perfect unity. What's judgment to the unbeliever is love to the believer. There's no disunity in God.

Second, all the persons of the Trinity are fully God. That means when the Spirit is leading us to do something, God is leading us. There's no division in God. When we read about Jesus, we're reading about God. In coming to Jesus with childlike faith, we're not avoiding the angry God of the Old Testament. This *is* God. To come to Jesus is to come into a living relationship with the triune God.

Keeping the oneness of God in mind simplifies a lot of things that could lead us to sketchy views of God. Every characteristic of God is in perfect harmony with every other characteristic or attribute of God. We might summarize this by saying simply, "God is God."

Third, these truths remind us that God doesn't change. If God isn't divided, God in the first century is the same as God in the twenty-first century. God is the same yesterday, today, and forever (Hebrews 13:8). We can sleep in peace at night knowing the God we served today will be trustworthy tomorrow and every day after that until the end of time and beyond.

Let's unpack this a little more. There's no God of last week who accepted you because of your faith in Jesus, versus a God of this week who now loves you less because you didn't read your Bible this morning. If God doesn't change, that means he will never change the way he feels about you. Because of poor decisions, you might not sense his love in the same way. That doesn't mean his love has changed, though. You will always be able to depend on him because there is no shadow of turning in him (James 1:17).

There's no future fact that God might learn about you that will make him regret saving you. Since God doesn't change, that means he doesn't learn new information. He isn't processing things like we are. He knows everything.

We aren't adding to God's knowledge every time we make a decision. Although I would argue we do make real decisions. I would also argue that God already knows what decisions we'll make. God knows every future fact about you, and if you're a Christian, he still decided to save you. You can't trick God into loving you when he knows every-thing about you.

Speaking of what's true of you, the Bible isn't silent on this topic either. We started this book arguing we need to form our theology by beginning with Scripture and working to understand the world and our place in it. In the next chapter, we'll turn our attention to the bookends of Scripture, the beginning and the end, to better understand our place in the in-between.

Questions for Reflection

1. How does the fact God is one help us understand the doctrine of the Trinity?
2. How does the Bible's teaching about God never changing help us understand passages that make it seem like God is changing?
3. In what ways does God having perfect and complete knowledge encourage you?
4. Is there a future action you could do that might surprise God or make him love you any less?
5. How do you feel about the tension between what the Bible says about God being in complete control and humans making real decisions?

SECTION 3

God's World

Mere Creation

*I love to think of nature as an unlimited
broadcasting station, through which God speaks
to us every hour, if we will only tune in.*
—GEORGE WASHINGTON CARVER

So far we've covered what the Bible says about itself and about God. Now we're going to look at what Scripture has to say about the world. When the stream of orthodoxy flows through the doctrine of creation, it's bounded on one side by the original creation of Genesis 1 and on the other side by the new creation of Revelation 21. Both images are ideal in many ways, but the new creation represents the completion of all things, the very culmination of God's saving work in the world. In keeping these two pictures in mind, we will better understand our world and our place in it.

To be clear, the garden motif in Scripture is about more than a fenced patch of land in your backyard where your parents grow tomatoes and carrots. In the Bible, the garden of Eden was to be expanded, to fill the whole earth (Genesis 1:28–29). The first couple were commanded to expand Eden from the inside out. That changed of course once they were placed on the outside. But the Bible is filled with visions of the Creator coming to make all things new.

In the new creation, the garden is transformed into a lavish city for all the people of God to live in. But these two pictures of God's dwelling place with humanity, the garden of Eden in the Old Testament and the new creation in the book of Revelation, provide bookends to the big story of redemption in the Bible.

If you held in your hands the pages of the Bible that deal with these two events—the original creation, and the new creation—you'd see that they make up the introduction and conclusion of the Bible. If you have a Bible nearby, try this on your own. Hold the pages of Genesis 1–2 with your left hand. Now hold the pages with Revelation 21–22 with your right hand. As you can see, the bulk of the Bible is in between. In fact, if you tore these sections out—these few pages of Scripture—then closed your Bible back up, there wouldn't be a perceptible change in size. Anyone glancing over at your Bible wouldn't notice anything had been removed.

If you did that, and I certainly don't encourage you to, you would remove both the explanation of and hope for our world. These passages seem insignificant in terms of the number of words and space they take up, but these beginning and ending themes permeate both testaments like a kudzu vine overtaking a landscape. You can't get away from them. But most of the Bible is situated in this in-between world, the one we know and inhabit, where sin looms large and despair often seems like it's going to win. Most of the Bible is about how to flourish in this fallen world.

How do you think the world has been affected by sin? Have you ever considered the promises in Scripture that say God is going to make all things new? But before we can consider the hope of a new creation, how Jesus is reversing the curse of sin, we have to consider the effects of Adam's and Eve's disobedience. As we'll see in this chapter, the stream of orthodoxy runs between these two banks—the original creation and the coming new creation.

Finally, we'll also ponder that age-old question of what it means to be human. It's only considering what God has revealed about himself that we can understand who we are. Only when we properly understand who he is, can we understand his world and our place in it. So let's get started by going back to the beginning.

On Reading Genesis

It's amazing what you can import into your reading of the Bible. We sometimes assume certain things are there, partially because they have been repeated to us so often. But when we go back to the text of Scripture to investigate it for ourselves, at times we can be surprised when we try to defend our beliefs. When it comes to creation, this can certainly be the case. We all have baggage, and we bring it with us when we read the Bible.

Making a list

One of the things I like to have my students do when we study creation is to get in groups and read over the first two chapters of Genesis. I have them make a list of things we can learn about the creation of the world from this short passage. The only rule is that they must be able to defend every single item on their list with the text of Genesis 1–2. If they offer a belief that's not clearly in the text, it doesn't make the list.

To be fair, the Bible talks about the creation in multiple places throughout the Bible (see Exodus 20:11, Job 10:9, Psalm 8:3, 33:6, and 102:25, for starters). That means our theology of creation is taken from the whole of Scripture. But for this exercise, I limit my students' assignment to the opening chapters of Genesis. I call this exercise "Mere Creation."

I'll have students share and defend their list. I'll write the items on the board that pass the test of being clear in the text. My students are at a bit of a disadvantage in this, since I only give them about thirty or forty-five minutes in class to complete the exercise. In a later lecture I share my own list with them. For you, I'll include my list below.

My list might surprise you. My goal is not to exhaust what the Bible says about creation, but to limit our preliminary thoughts on creation based merely on what's evident in Genesis 1–2. If you're new to the doctrine of creation, you should probably know that Christians can differ greatly on how to best understand this first part of Genesis.

Understanding the views

On the one hand, you have Christians who feel it's best to take everything in the text as literally as possible. Then, on the other hand, there are Christians who see something else in the passage, something like a poetic description of the origin of the world that's not intended to be taken literally. Since we're talking about orthodoxy, it's important to note this is a topic that sincere and orthodox Christians can disagree on in finer points and still be unified in their belief in Jesus.

As you will see in my list that follows, I take a more literal reading of Genesis. That doesn't mean I take it all literally. I don't think anyone does or should. It's more complicated than that.

Not everything in the first two chapters of Genesis is intended to be taken literally. We've mentioned one already, the description of God "walking" in the garden. Another

148

example we'll look at later is the language about Adam and Eve being created in God's image. If you only considered a literal interpretation of the expression of image, you might conclude that Adam and Eve looked like God. That would be the most literal reading of the text.

Since God doesn't have a body, the literal reading of that expression can't be right. If you read the language of God walking and talking with Adam and Eve, or that they were made in God's image, in a literal way, you could easily form a sketchy view of God. You could assume God has a body and that Adam and Eve were made to resemble him in some physical way. That's why I prefer to say I take the Bible seriously instead of saying I take it literally.

As I said, not everything in the Bible is intended to be read as literal. When the psalmist says the "hills are skipping like calves," he's not giving a scientific observation. There are places in Scripture where reading the Bible well requires us to take a deeper look at what's going on in the passage. The way we interpret the Bible needs to be carefully nuanced and properly grounded in the text of Scripture. And there are few places where that's more challenging than the beginning and ending of the Bible—Genesis and Revelation.

Yet our guiding principle is unity in the essential things, liberty in the nonessential things, and charity in all things. Every Christian should seek to formulate a view of creation that's based on what they feel is the most faithful reading of the text. The important question to ask is what does the text demand? What does faithfulness to God, as he's revealed himself, require from us as good Bible readers?

Although I've provided my own list below, my goal is for you to read the text of Scripture carefully yourself. I want you to come to your own conclusions faithful to God's Word. So let's pretend you're in my theology class at the university. Grab a Bible and open it to Genesis. Take a break from this book to read the first two chapters. Make your own list of basic details. Again, if you can't find it in the text of Genesis 1–2, don't include it on your list.

Mere Creation

The Bible doesn't begin with a philosophical argument for God's existence. It merely asserts God made everything. "In the beginning God created the heavens and the earth," Moses writes in the first verse of the Bible. The expression "the heavens and the earth" is a way of saying "everything." It's a statement of totality.

I like to tell my students that the main point of every creation passage in the Bible is twofold. God is the author of the world and its owner. He made it all. He owns it all. No matter how Christians differ on how to best read Genesis, they can and should agree on God's authorship and owner- ship of all things.

My list below is not intended to be exhaustive. There are a lot more details we can unpack in the first two chapters of Genesis. You'll likely have more things on your list than I give below. But I think this is a good place to begin.

1. God made everything.

The Bible uses the Hebrew term for create, *bara,* in a unique way for God's creative activity. In the first verse of the Bible, this term is used to describe how God created everything out of nothing. There's a Latin term *ex nihilo* theologians use to express this belief. In the beginning, there was no preexisting stuff, like matter and energy, that God used to make his world.

Christians aren't saying everything came from nothing; rather, God made everything and he didn't use anything to make it. God's not like an artist today, who must always work with preexisting materials like wood, stone, paper, or paint. He's not like one of my kids who builds something out of Legos. God used no things to make our world, which is just another way to say he made it out of nothing.

2. God's Spirit is actively involved in creation.

I sometimes have students jump the gun by saying we get introduced to the Trinity in Genesis 1–2. I appreciate their enthusiasm, but we really don't a full-orbed teaching of the Trinity here. We get something very interesting about this Creator God. He talks to himself, saying things like, "Let us make man in our image." This much is also clear—God's Spirit is active in creation (Genesis 1:2).

3. God's creation is sequential.

God could have made everything at once. He didn't. He begins by making the material universe (Genesis 1:1). His Spirit is then involved in shaping creation (1:2). But God isn't finished yet. The Hebrew term *bara* is used a total of five times in the first chapter of Genesis. In addition to its use in the first verse, it's used again when God creates conscious animal life (1:21) and three times when he creates human life (1:27).

4. God's preparation of the world took place over six days.

It's also important to note the obvious pattern of the "days" mentioned in the first chapter of Genesis. The Hebrew word for day is *yom*, and it's used in three different ways in the Old Testament: a twenty-four-hour day ("This day has been great"); the part of the day when the sun is up, daytime ("How was your day?"); or a longer period of time ("These are the days of the king").

YOM = DAY

In Genesis 1–2, there's a unique combination of terms or elements associated with the days. First, the Hebrew word *yom* mentioned above. Second, we have ordinals or numbering of the days, which we interpret as "day one," and "day two," and so on. Some people will say that if you have *yom* plus the numbering or ordinals, it must be interpreted as a twenty-four-hour period. But we find this same formulation in Hosea 6:2, where something other than a literal twenty-four-hour period seems to be expressed. Again, we want to let the Bible help us interpret the Bible and not rely upon forced solutions.

There's another element to how the days are described in the opening of Genesis—the addition of the expression "evening and morning." While the Hebrew word for day is used in different ways in the Old Testament, the creation passage in Genesis is the only place where these three elements are used together ([yom + ordinals] + "evening and morning" phrase). There's nowhere else in the Bible with this unique formulation.

Hebrew Word for Day in Genesis 1

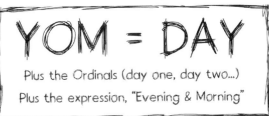

YOM = DAY

Plus the Ordinals (day one, day two...)
Plus the expression, "Evening & Morning"

In trying to write our "Mere Creation" list, it doesn't take long to reach the limits of the text. While I think the best way to read the formula mentioned above regarding the six days of creation is to see them as real twenty-four-hour days, caution is advised. As Francis Schaeffer said in his book *Genesis in Space and Time*,[1] the data is too limited for us to be overly dogmatic on issues related to the days or the age of the earth.

That doesn't mean you can avoid forming an opinion. You're a theologian. You need to think about these things. Nevertheless, you should hold your conclusions with humility. And you should always be open to being persuaded otherwise by Scripture. The Bible is your authority, not merely some book by some author (including this one!).

5. God created every kind of living thing.

I remember a skeptic friend of mine trying to persuade me to believe in an evolutionary understanding of the origin of the diversity of life. As I looked into it, I was surprised to discover how much debate and disagreement there was among scientists about what constitutes one species and makes them different from another. My friend sent me an article he felt would settle the matter.

The article was about a species of salamanders whose migration pattern split the group into two sets. One group migrated to the sunny side of a mountain range. The other group migrated to the dark side of the mountain range that received little sunlight during the day. Over time, these groups reconnected. But the two groups were no longer able to mate and have offspring. The article concluded that this was now two species of salamanders because they could only mate within their particular group.

I won't argue the science. I'm not a scientist. I'm no expert on salamanders. But when the Bible says God made every sort of living thing, to produce after its "kind," whether botanical or animal life, I think it has in mind something much larger than our contemporary and technical use of the term *species*. The biblical category of "kind" seems far broader. I think it must capture every species of dog from a pit bull to the miniature Chihuahuas some celebrities carry about in their designer purses. The biblical category of kind certainly seems large enough to account for the salamanders my friend told me about.

My point is that there's an emphasis on God as the author of this diversity—from plants to animals. He made things as *kinds* of plants and *kinds* of animals. He said they would produce according to their *kinds* (Genesis 1:11, 12, 21, 24, 25). This is an important detail to consider when we think about the best model for making sense of Genesis.

6. God created humanity in his image.

In the first chapter we see that God made humanity in his image (Genesis 1:26–28). Their dignity was found in the fact that they were created in God's image and given dominion over God's creation. Theologians refer to this as the "special creation" of Adam and Eve to emphasize humans were directly formed by God, not just spoken into existence and not descended from other life-forms. As Dietrich Bonhoeffer points out in his book on Genesis, "There is no transition from somewhere else here; here there is new creation. This has nothing whatsoever to do with Darwin."[2]

Genesis 2 gives greater detail about Adam's and Eve's creation as male and female and how they serve as the model for all marriages (Genesis 2:22–24). In the last chapter of this book, we'll take a closer look at what it means be human, as those created in the image of the Creator. Theologians refer to this doctrine as *imago dei*, a Latin expression for *Image of God*.

Some Christians read Genesis as a poetic description compatible with an evolutionary understanding of common descent, that humans descended from preexisting life-forms. The burden of proof is on the person making such a claim. In our "Mere Creation" list, we don't have the option to make claims not clear in the text. In this way, a view promoting an evolutionary explanation of the origin of humanity has to argue for their position from somewhere other than Scripture, making something like scientific consensus the starting point for developing a theology of creation.

I often tell my students I don't feel compelled by either Scripture or science to accept an evolutionary view of humanity. I have Christian friends who hold such a position. I've never punched them in the face. I've never said nasty things about them for holding such a view. While they read Genesis in a far less straightforward way than I do, they still believe in the fallen condition of humanity and the historical sacrifice of Jesus. I can be charitable, even where I disagree, and I can recognize our shared commitment to Christ as the Savior of the world.

Nevertheless, I don't see how the evolutionary view flows from the text. I will concede this much to my friends who hold such a view: the creation account does begin with the material universe, and then there is a kind of progression from Day 3 to Day 6, from simple life-forms like plants, to more complex ones like animals, and finally to humans. For this reason, I understand why my friends don't see a conflict between the overarching claims of the Bible and evolution.

Nonetheless, I personally don't find sufficient evidence in the text to conclude it should be read as poetry or mythology. And I believe the text of Scripture should be the starting point and the authority. I think the evidence in the text points in the other direction, away from the evolution of humanity. But as I will explain, there are bits and pieces that can be difficult to completely understand from any model. As theologians, we must do our best to make sense of Scripture, asking God's Spirit to guide us in best interpreting and applying it.

7. God rested on the seventh day.

In Genesis 2, we see that God finished his work and then rested on the seventh day. If you've been paying attention in earlier chapters, you might recognize this as *anthropomorphic* language. God is never tired. He's never drowsy. He never slumbers nor sleeps (Psalm 121:4).

Nothing drains his energy, not even creating a world. There must be something else going on. It seems God's rest signifies he finished his creative activity in our material universe. And this rhythm of work and rest also serves as a model for us in working six days and resting on the seventh (Exodus 20:8–11).

There's also another interesting point here. The seventh day breaks the formula. We have the Hebrew word for day, and we have the ordinals, but the phrase "evening and morning" is conspicuously missing. Theologians reason this seventh day is not a twenty-four-hour period, but rather, that God has now eternally rested from his creation in our material universe. God is no longer actively creating in our world.

While our remembrance of the Sabbath day is a twenty-four-hour period, it doesn't seem in the text that God's sabbath rest is a mere twenty-four hours (Hebrews 4:9). We use a literal day, the Sabbath, to remember the day God rested, a day which doesn't seem to be a literal twenty-four-hour period.

Bits and Pieces

Several years ago, I wrote a book through a publisher based in London, England. My editor was extremely helpful. We came from very different life experiences. I had grown up in very conservative, some would say "fundamentalist," churches. She's grew up in a non-Christian family. I'm married. She's single. I'm American. She's British. I'm Baptist. She's Anglican. To top it off, we're a good decade apart in terms of life stage.

She would often send me edits for my book with the email subject line "some bits and pieces." I'd always laugh when I saw that. I think it was her way of telling me there was some stuff she didn't quite get or like in my manuscript. It always meant I had some editing to do.

When it comes to Genesis, I think there are some bits and pieces that don't fully make sense. To be clear, I don't mean Moses wasn't inspired in writing Genesis, or that the Holy Spirit has some editing to do. I simply mean these bits and pieces don't perfectly fit into any model of creation. That's not to say some models aren't better than others. It *is* to say all of them have certain tension points.

Because I'm trying to persuade you to let the Bible be your starting point for theology, I think it's important to model what it looks like to really wrestle with a passage of Scripture, rather than just glossing over the details. Let me outline some bits and pieces to hopefully show you some of the challenges to forming a position.

In my humble but accurate opinion (insert smiley emoticon), no one model can resolve every issue. And it's very likely that someone smarter than me can come up with even more bits and pieces in this passage. Maybe they can even figure out how to fully explain them from a single model. I haven't been able to yet. I'm just trying to keep it real.

First, how exactly do we understand what Genesis 1:1 means when it says that God created everything ("the heavens and the earth")? Should that first verse be considered like a title or summary statement so that what follows is just a description of what he created? Is there a time gap between verse one and what follows? Or is the creation of the universe a separate event that happened before the six days of God's specific creative activity related to the earth and the garden of Eden? It seems to read that way, which is how I take it. It's clear Genesis 1:1 describes the first day of the universe, but is it also the first day of the first week?

Some Christians, who hold a view known as *young earth creationism*, say Genesis 1:1 is a title. But if it's just a title, then that introduces a pretty big issue, in my opinion. If "In the beginning God created the heavens and the earth" is a title, then the very first act of creation we find in Genesis is the Spirit of God hovering over some kind of preexisting water. Those who hold such a position don't believe matter is eternal, but if we reduce the first verse of the Bible to a title, then we no longer have the creation of everything out of nothing being taught in the first chapter of Genesis (see also Hebrews 11:3).

In contrast, some theologians have argued there's a gap between God's original creation in verse one and what follows. It's not surprisingly called "The Gap Theory." They reason that the first verse of Genesis is not a title; it's a separate event. This debate is understandable because Genesis 1:1 does demand some kind of explanation. In other words, it's not immediately clear without further thought and reflection. You need some sort of system to make sense of it.

One Bible teacher even went so far as to suggest that Satan is responsible for the world being "without form" in verse 2. God made it all in verse 1, they argued, and then Satan made a mess of things. Then enter the Holy Spirit in verse 2. The Spirit hovers over the waters and reorganizes it all.

In that view, between verses 1 and 2, Satan is created, he sins and falls, leads a bunch of angels to join him, and together they muck up the world. That's a whole lot to load into the space between two verses! Again, if we can't find it in the text, we can't put it on our "Mere Creation" list.

Second, another issue that can be hard to resolve is how the vegetation could sprout and the trees bear fruit on day three (Genesis 1:11–13) when the sun isn't created until day four (Genesis 1:14–19). As you likely know from your school biology classes, these growth processes require photosynthesis, and you can't get that without the sun. Surely God could have just made them grow without the sun. Of course! After all, God is the author and owner of all things. Nonetheless, this is just one of those bits and pieces careful readers will notice and take into account.

Third, if you read about the creation of humanity in Genesis 2, it's interesting to compare it to the description of the creation of humanity on the sixth day in Genesis 1. These two accounts of creation—Genesis 1 and Genesis 2—are very different. If you have a Bible nearby, check it out for yourselves. If we didn't have Genesis 1, and all we had was the second chapter, we would think the creation of Adam and Eve was separated by far more than a day. Let me explain.

Consider the details of Genesis 2 without looking back at Genesis 1. The events of Genesis 2 are as follows: The earth did not yet have vegetation or fruit-bearing trees, and there was no one to tend the land (2:5). God creates Adam (2:7). God plants a garden in Eden and places Adam in it (2:8). God causes all the vegetation and trees to grow and bear fruit (2:9). It's then restated that God places Adam in the garden (2:15). God says it's not good for the man to be alone (2:18). God creates the animals and has Adam name them (2:19). God causes a deep sleep to fall over Adam and takes one of Adam's ribs to form Eve (2:21–22). Upon waking up, Adam sees Eve and declares, "This one, at last, is bone of my bone and flesh of my flesh; this one will be called 'woman,' for she was taken from man" (2:23).

If we didn't have Genesis 1 with the clear distinction between days, we would likely read this as being a long period of time. We see a season—however long or short—preceding God planting the garden and creating Adam. How long might it take Adam to study and name all the animals? Why does Adam's expression seem to imply a lengthy time period without Eve, when, upon first seeing her, he declares "at last," finally, here was someone like him?

There are some other bits and pieces in Genesis that can raise your eyebrow. For example, in the first chapter, animals are created before humans, but that order is reversed in Genesis 2. I think there is a good explanation of this, and I clearly don't believe Moses is so incompetent he didn't realize the differences between the two chapters he wrote. There must be a purpose for how God inspired him to write these two descriptions in Genesis. Yet it's easy to find perplexing questions that might not easily fit into any system that attempts to make sense of creation.

What Do We Make of God's Making?

So what are some ways to pull all this together? I've tried to show you that no model is going to perfectly account for everything. There are tension points for each way of trying to make sense of the opening chapters of the Bible. There's enough going on in early Genesis to show us we need to be careful that we don't quickly label someone as sketchy for sincerely struggling to understand it. The main point is

God's authorship and ownership. But that's not to say there aren't some models that can or should be considered better or more faithful than others.

I've not said much about reading the creation account as symbolic or poetic. There are believers who love God and affirm the authority of the Bible and see Genesis as such. If you're interested in reading an analysis that compares such views, check out John Lennox's helpful book *Seven Days That Divide the World.*[3]

One last thing before we move on. I aspire to be charitable toward Christians who adopt the evolutionary view of Genesis—that God made the world and its natural processes in order to eventually bring about life in all its diversity, culminating in humanity. Yet I personally don't see this position as flowing from the text of Scripture. For anyone wanting to do a deep dive on a response to theistic evolution, I commend the book *Theistic Evolution: A Scientific, Philosophical, and Theological Critique* published by Crossway Books.[4] Just a warning—it's not short.

Be a Bible-Loving Berean

In the book of Acts there was a group of believers known by where they were from: Berea. The book of Acts says these "Berean" believers were more noble than others because they went back and studied the Scriptures for themselves to verify what Paul was preaching (17:11). When it came to understanding God, they wouldn't just take someone else's position. They went back to the Bible and studied it for themselves. That's my encouragement for you.

Be like the Bereans. Study the Bible for yourself, and ask the Spirit for guidance in how to best understand and apply it. Seek to prioritize what the Bible prioritizes. If the stream of orthodoxy flows first from Scripture and then to our experience in the world, then we don't want to reverse things. We don't want to start with modern science and try to make the Bible fit what we find. Nor do we want to make some current Christian leader the authority. Trust the Bible as your authority.

Every semester I give my students a class period in which to watch a lecture about the Bible by the late theologian R. C. Sproul. I also have them read a document called "The Chicago Statement on Biblical Inerrancy," which Sproul helped write. Then I have my students write a response to both the video and the statement. We do this early in the semester, but there's a detail from this assignment that I don't point out until the end of the semester when we talk about creation.

In one of my final lectures, I will have a bit of a *Karate Kid* moment. If you've seen the movie, you probably know what I'm talking about. The film is about a young man named Daniel who learns karate from an older gentleman named Mr. Miyagi. Daniel begins his training with a whole lot of physical labor like painting a fence, sanding a floor, and waxing old cars. When Daniel has had enough of this busy work, Mr. Miyagi finally lets him in on the method to his madness.

"Paint the fence," he tells Daniel. When his student makes the painting motion, Mr. Miyagi throws a punch that's blocked by Daniel's hand moving in an upward motion. "Sand the floor," the teacher tells him, as Daniel blocks a kick. It's at this point that Daniel learns the lessons behind the busy-work assignments.[5]

So, my *Karate Kid* moment is when I tell my class one of the big reasons I had them read "The Chicago Statement on Biblical Inerrancy" when we were talking about the doctrine of Scripture. I'm sure they all assumed it was only because the statement was about the Bible. At the end of the semester, I explain to them I had them read it for the doctrine of creation as well. Here's why:

The scholars who compiled the statement differ among themselves about how to best read Genesis. Some of them believed the earth was really old. Some of them believed it was really young. Still others didn't feel the Bible offered a way to have any certainty about the age of the earth. But all the scholars were unified in their love for the Bible. They modeled for us what it looks like to pursue unity in essential things, liberty in nonessential things, and charity in all things.

Let's follow their example.

Questions for Reflection

1. What did you have on your "Mere Creation" list?
2. How was your list different from mine?
3. Did you discover any beliefs you assumed were based on the text of Scripture but really weren't?

Our World Fallen

But in the end, it's only a passing thing, this shadow;
even darkness must pass.

—J. R. R. TOLKIEN

Imagine how beautiful the original creation must have been. If the world today, though under a veil of a curse, is still so breathtaking, what must the original creation have been like? If we look at our fallen world and think it's amazing, what do you think it must have meant for God, the Creator, to step back and call his creation "very good" (Genesis 1:31)? That's high praise from the highest authority of all.

God is a good gardener. "The LORD God planted a garden in Eden, in the east, and there he placed the man he had formed," Moses tells us (Genesis 2:8). The next verse distinguishes between the kinds of trees God had made. It says God made some trees for fruit and some simply to be pleasing to the sight (Genesis 2:9). God made a good world that was just right for human life to flourish in his presence.

Isn't it interesting though, how the Bible gives specific details about the two trees God placed in the garden, the "Tree of Knowledge of Good and Evil" and the "Tree of

Life"? Have you ever given much thought to what's going on there? What might these trees mean?

Two Trees, One Choice

I used to think that the Tree of Knowledge of Good and Evil—the one Adam and Eve weren't supposed to eat from—was kind of like my parents going on a trip and leaving me at home alone when I was a teenager. God telling Adam and Eve they could eat from any tree except this particular one always felt random to me. Why this tree?

It would be like my parents leaving me the credit card, the keys to the car, a bunch of cash, and telling me I could do whatever I wanted while they were gone, except I was not supposed to drink the Diet Coke in the refrigerator. With all I was allowed to do, how would this solitary thing that seems so insignificant be a point of stumbling?

The same is true in Genesis. In the untarnished splendor of God's custom-designed garden, who cares about a solitary tree? Yet the single decision to eat fruit from this forbidden tree is responsible for why we have mass shootings, kids get cancer, parents get divorced, storms wreak havoc to communities, and every human being lives in the shadow of death all their days. All because of this one tree? Really?

So we need to think carefully about this tree. If we read these first two chapters of Genesis with attention to detail, we can get a good idea of what's going on. Moses establishes a pattern in his description of creation. In Genesis 1, we see God repeatedly calls his handiwork "good" (Genesis 1:4, 10, 12, 18, 21, 25, 31). Then in Genesis 2, we read that God notes one thing isn't good: Adam doesn't have a suitable mate (Genesis 2:18). Here again we see it is God who identifies what is good and what isn't good. That's God's prerogative. It's God's moral authority.

The Tree of Knowledge of Good and Evil could also be translated, perhaps more helpfully so, as the "Tree of Knowledge of Good and Not Good." By the way, when I mentioned the verse that says God made some trees for fruit and some for sight, I did so to try to help you pay attention to what's going on in the passage. The verse also describes the two trees we've been discussing, the Tree of Life and the "Tree of Knowledge of Good and Not Good" (Genesis 2:9). The Tree of Life was one of the many trees they could eat from. The "Tree of Knowledge of Good and Not Good" may have had fruit, but because of God's command, it was only for sight. They could look at it but not eat from it.

Adam and Eve could eat from the Tree of Life all they wanted. But with the "Tree of Knowledge of Good and Not Good," they could only admire its grandeur but never taste its fruit. To be clear, I believe it was a real tree. The text makes that rather clear.

I think this real tree symbolized God's moral authority. God is the one who decides what is good and what is not good. Adam and Eve could live in the harmony of God's good creation by eating freely from the Tree of Life and by spending their days within the majesty of God's good design, under God's moral authority. They could eat, and they could see, and they could live.

A Natural Disaster

God also tells Adam and Eve that if they did eat from the tree of knowledge, in the day they ate from it, they would die (Genesis 2:17). This statement can be a bit confusing. As you may have noticed, Adam and Eve eventually eat from the forbidden tree in Genesis 3. And yet they live to see chapter 4, and they even make it all the way to chapter 5, where we learn Adam doesn't die until he's 930 years old. What's up with that?

Several years ago, I led the office of public relations and communications at The Southern Baptist Theological Seminary, a graduate school in Louisville, Kentucky. The president of the school is an influential scholar named Albert Mohler, who has considerable influence among Christians and non-Christians alike. *Time* magazine once described him as the intellectual leader of evangelical Christians in America. To lead a department responsible for his communications was every bit as intimidating as it might sound. I survived.

To be honest, I really enjoyed my time in that role. Dr. Mohler made regular media appearances and even hosted a daily nationally syndicated radio program. Every week he would have one episode devoted to questions and answers from callers. It was called "Ask Anything Wednesdays." It was never predictable. You never knew who was going to call in or what they might ask. And it was never boring.

At an anniversary dinner where the school was honoring Dr. Mohler for his years of service at the school, his grown daughter gave a memorable speech. She described how as a young girl she always wondered how Adam and Eve didn't die on the same day they ate the fruit, as God had told them they would. She was afraid to ask because it seemed no one else had noticed. Since her dad was so influential, she didn't want to, well, mess things up and point out this glaring contradiction she alone had discovered, and thus somehow destroy the church. She didn't want to make her father question the reliability of the Bible.

So one day she disguised her voice, used a different name, and called into the radio program. She asked her question anonymously. When her father came home later that day, she commented about the insightful caller who asked about Adam and Eve. Her dad said something to the effect of, "Yeah, it really wasn't that thoughtful of a question," and went about his business.

At the celebration dinner years after the incident, for the first time ever, she shared with her dad that she was the caller. People were literally crying as they laughed out loud. As you might imagine, no one was more affected by the story than her father, Dr. Mohler. He was crying he was laughing so hard.

The reality is, however, that Dr. Mohler's daughter isn't alone. This is a question many of us have pondered. Sadly, the answer we're often given overlooks the reality of the text. Often people will point out that Adam and Eve began dying that same day, the process of death started that very moment. But God didn't tell them they would *begin* dying. He told them they would die in the day they ate the fruit. How do we make sense of that?

We can get clarity for this by reading the New Testament. For example, in Ephesians 2, the apostle Paul describes those who don't have a relationship with God as being spiritually dead. I think it's best to understand the Genesis passage in the same way. Adam and Eve actually died on the day they ate from the tree of knowledge. Deep on the inside, a part of them no one could see but no one could deny, died. The souls created to flourish in God's presence were now dead. God's good design had turned sour.

When Adam and Eve took fruit from the tree symbolizing God's moral authority, they were saying, "God will not be God over us. We can determine what is good for ourselves." They made themselves like God by claiming authority to determine what was good and not good.

You and I have done the same thing on more occasions than we care to admit. We're not unfamiliar with spiritual death. It wasn't an arbitrary tree. It wasn't insignificant fruit. It was a picture of God's rule and reign as king of the world. Adam and Eve didn't want that kind of king.

You can *listen* and learn (and avoid difficult consequences), or you can *live* and learn (by experiencing those consequences). Sadly, we all tend to learn the hard way. The entire Old Testament is a commentary on how bad humans are at figuring out what's good and what's not good. We take something good and we call it evil. We take something evil and we call it good (Isaiah 5:20).

God's moral authority is not opposed to human flourishing. It's the path of life. Yet still, like that first couple in the garden, we too have a fatal attraction for forbidden fruit. And we know what it's like to be dead on the inside too.

The Problem of Evil

A few years ago, I wrote a book about the effects of the fall of the human race described in Genesis 3. It's called *Life in the Wild: Fighting for Faith in a Fallen World*.[1] It would be worth your time to make a list of all your observations of the fall based only on Genesis 3, like we did in the last chapter with Genesis 1–2.

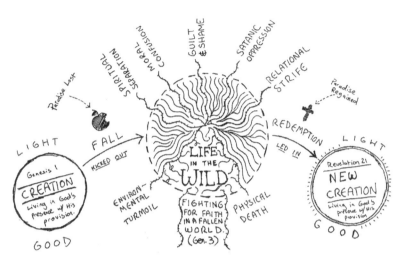

My book was really the result of a message I shared with college students many years before, when I was asked to talk about what is described as "the problem of evil." This problem centers on this question: how can we believe in a good God, when the world is filled with so much sin and suffering?

Instead of starting out with helpful philosophical arguments, I thought I would simply go to Genesis and ask what we should expect the world to be like outside of Eden if what the Bible says is true. So I turned to Genesis 3 in my Bible, got out a notepad, and began making a list of my own. I suggest you take a break from reading here and go and do that for yourself. Make your own list of the effects of the fall from Genesis 3.

In the book, I asked these questions: *Does the way the world is somehow disprove the God of the Bible, or does it line up with what it feels like to be alive in the world? Does evil and suffering disprove God?* When it comes to evil, scholars normally think about two different kinds of evil. There is natural evil and moral evil. Natural evil is when something bad happens like a tornado or earthquake or a tree falling on someone's house. These are the kinds of events where there's no human effort or agency. Now if someone intentionally cut down the tree so it would fall on someone else's house that would be a different kind of evil. It would be moral evil because there is human intention behind it.

We see both natural evil and moral evil all around us. When someone says they can't believe in the God of the Bible because of all the evil in the world, these are the kind of categories they have in mind. There are natural disasters, and there are moral monsters in the world. Where is God in it all?

I find that the Bible offers an amazingly accurate description of what humans should expect in life outside of Eden. The Bible accounts for natural evil. Adam is told the land is now under a curse (Genesis 3:17–19). The Bible also accounts for moral evil. Outside the garden, sin is described as "crouching at the door," with a desire to dominate us (Genesis 4:7). The Bible makes sense of what we see in the newspapers every day. And it makes sense of what we see in the mirror.

The Bible makes sense of the evil out there. And it makes sense of the evil in here—deep in our hearts where there's an evil that lures us away from God's design, that causes us to choose evil over goodness. I love how theologian Nels F. S. Ferré summed it up, "It is precisely because the Christian faith solves the problem of evil with amazing adequacy that I have become so convinced a Christian. It solves evil in thought; it solves evil in life."[2]

The Bible not only offers a category for evil, it provides a solution. If a person rejects belief in God because of the sin and suffering in the world, because of what's called the problem of evil, they're not going to find a better explanation elsewhere. In fact, alternative explanations are much worse.

The Reality of Evil

There are a number of secular authors like the celebrated atheistic author Richard Dawkins, or Duke University philosophy professor and atheist Alex Rosenberg, who admit that if there is no God, there is no basis for good and evil. If there is no God, we have nothing but "blind pitiless indifference" to quote Richard Dawkins.[3] Or as Rosenberg says, the idea of moral distinctions, to call one thing good and another evil, is simply an illusion.[4]

C. S. Lewis discovered this contradiction in his own atheism. Early in life, he rejected God because the universe was so unjust. But the more he thought about it, the more he realized that without God, there would be no standard for justice. How could we call one thing good and another thing evil if we have no standard beyond our own opinions and preferences? We can say we don't *like* certain things, but that's far from a real statement that a thing is actually wrong. For example, you might subjectively prefer vanilla ice cream to chocolate, but that doesn't prove anything objectively true for everyone else.

There are plenty of people like Dawkins or Rosenberg who reject belief in God because of evil in the world, but having rejected God, they also go on to reject the idea of evil too. It's a bit ironic. It's also a self-defeating exercise. In order to be consistent, Lewis said he either had to come back to belief in God, or he had to let go of his idea of justice. He chose the former and turned in faith to the Creator.

Genesis 3 is packed with insights about the sad state of affairs outside of the garden. We see that the curse of sin brings about spiritual death, moral confusion, guilt and shame, spiritual warfare, relational disharmony, environmental turmoil, and in time, physical death as well. I included a sketch I made to illustrate the effects of the fall from Genesis 3.

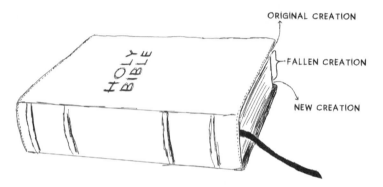

In the same way we often assume certain beliefs about creation are clear in Genesis 1–2, I've found we tend to smuggle some stuff into Genesis 3 as well. For example, I remember years ago sitting in a Bible class in college where my professor described what Adam and Eve looked like. They were bright pink, he told us. They didn't have dead skin cells, since there was no death in the garden.

I had never heard that before. They had no hair or nails because what we see above the skin's surface is made up of dead cells, he told us. The first couple sounded hideous, by the way. My professor's assumption isn't as uncommon as I first thought, at least in regard to the statement that there was no form of death whatsoever in the garden. But does the text ever say that there was no death of any kind in Eden?

Both the Old and New Testaments focus on human death resulting from the curse (Genesis 3; 1 Corinthians 15:20–22). Genesis doesn't say anything about other forms of death. And I think it's a stretch to say the lack of human death before the fall means Adam and Eve were bright red and bald. Furthermore, does the Bible say anything about heat death, plant death, animal death? Genesis doesn't say.

Having said all that, we want to be careful not to build an argument from silence, assuming something is true just because there isn't a clear contradictory statement. Maybe they really didn't have hair or nails. I don't know. But we also need to be honest when our beliefs aren't based on what's clear in the text. In my professor's case, he presented his view as if it was as certain as the ink on the page.

One thing is for certain—the relationship Adam and Eve enjoyed with God was severed, portrayed by their eviction from the garden. Now that Adam and Eve no longer had access to the Tree of Life, their physical bodies would slowly catch up with the sad state of their souls. Their bodies, no longer sustained by God's provision in God's presence, would slowly die as well. Just as the author of Hebrews tells us, it is appointed for every person to one day die and then face God's judgment (Hebrews 9:27).

I love the way German pastor and author Dietrich Bonhoeffer summarizes Adam and Eve's exile from the garden of Eden: "Humankind no longer lives in the beginning; instead, it has lost the beginning. Now it finds itself in the middle, knowing neither the end nor the beginning, and yet knowing that it is in the middle. It knows therefore that it comes from the beginning and must move on toward the end. It sees its life as determined by these two factors . . . ."[5]

Once they tasted the forbidden fruit, there was no going back. Eden was merely a speed bump at the beginning of the human journey. Paradise was lost. But a promise made in the garden can light our path forward. God's promise to send a child to defeat the serpent is our only hope (Genesis 3:15).

We will never go back, but we must move forward. To paraphrase C. S. Lewis, there are rumors of something even better rustling about in the pages of the New Testament. We see hints of it all throughout the Bible. There's another garden in our future. There's a new and better Eden awaiting.

God, the Good Gardener

Eden was a place of perfect peace, where humans lived in the presence of God and were satisfied with his provision— until that dreadful day when they rebelled. They turned away from God's good design to determine for themselves what was good. And did they ever make a mess of things! C. S. Lewis described history as "the long terrible story of man trying to find something other than God which will make him happy."[6]

Thankfully, the landscape of the Old Testament is blossoming with glimpses of grace and budding with garden imagery. Though we live in the middle, to use Bonhoeffer's term, we look forward to the end. The Bible points us to a future reality where humanity can again dwell with God. But it's not a safe or easy path. It's a long road back, covered with thorns and thistles and haunted by lions and tigers and bears. Oh my!

Once again, we find ourselves between the banks of this part of the stream of orthodoxy, with the original design of creation on one side, and the promises of a new creation on the other. If our theology teaches us anything, things will indeed get much worse before they get better. Yet there's a ray of hope piercing the darkness of this fallen world. This reality is glimmering on the surface of the stream of orthodoxy: God hasn't left us to face a fallen world on our own.

God is the Good Shepherd who leads us from green pastures and still waters all the way through the valley of the shadow of death (Psalm 23). Even as we are surrounded by enemies on every side, God's prepares a table for us. He gives us a feast even in the middle of the wilderness. His goodness and mercy will never leave us, and the Shepherd will lead us all the way home. As exiles from Eden, we can have hope.

I've always felt the twenty-third Psalm gives an impressively accurate panoramic view of the Christian life. Take a moment and read it now. It will take less than a minute.

> The LORD is my shepherd;
> I have what I need.
> He lets me lie down in green pastures;
> He leads me beside quiet waters.
> He renews my life;
> He leads me along the right paths
> for his name's sake.
> Even when I go through the darkest valley,
> I fear no danger,
> for you are with me;
> your rod and your staff—they comfort me.
> You prepare a table before me
> in the presence of my enemies;
> you anoint my head with oil;
> my cup overflows.
> Only goodness and faithful love will pursue me
> all the days of my life,
> and I will dwell in the house of the LORD
> as long as I live. (Psalm 23)

When I read this psalm, I always want to stay in the opening verses. I'd rather live in green pastures and enjoy still waters than face enemies and death. But God is over the whole story. He's the author and the owner. He's the shepherd who's with us, comforting us with his staff, prodding us along, protecting and directing us all the way to the end. We need that kind of leadership and love out here in the wild.

Even though Adam and Eve had to leave the garden, God never left his people. God's people couldn't go back to Eden, but that didn't mean God couldn't come to them. We live in this fallen world in light of the promise that God, our Good Shepherd, is leading us through the valley of the shadow of death right into the new creation, from one garden into another.

Think about the event when Moses went up the mountain to receive the Ten Commandments. God gave his people the law, and he also gave them a tent. The tent was called the tabernacle. It was the place God provided for his people to go for forgiveness when they broke the law. That's grace. It had to be a tent because they were a people on the run. They were exiles in the world. In a lot of ways, we've all been running since the first couple was exiled from Eden.

In days of old, one day of the year, every year, God's presence would descend to the tabernacle. That's when this portable tent was like a miniature, mobile version of the garden of Eden. God's presence was again there with his people. The high priest was able to stand in God's presence in a similar way that Adam and Eve once walked with God (Leviticus 16).

Later when the children of Israel settled down, they built a permanent tabernacle they called the temple. Both its construction and finished structure were dripping with grace. The person to build the temple was Solomon, whose father was King David and whose mother was Bathsheba.

If you know the story of David and Bathsheba, you'll know that a child born to their troubled marriage might seem an unlikely candidate to construct a building devoted to God's presence. But isn't that the way God works? He takes our brokenness and offers us himself. He forgives. He heals. He leads.

If you read the instructions for how they were to build the tabernacle and temple, you'll see there's a lot of botanical imagery. I think that's because these structures reflected the garden of Eden, where God lived in harmony with his people.

God manifested his presence in these places in a similar way as he walked in the garden. This is a reminder of what humanity was created for. The tabernacle and the temple are pointing us back to the original garden and forward to the better garden that is yet to come. Yet the imagery of a garden can't be contained within the walls of the temple.

A Garden Tour of the Bible

The Bible and our own experiences resonate with garden imagery. Our first ancestors were created in a glorious garden, the original garden of Eden. And yet for us, Eden is a million miles away. It's a dim memory and a locked mystery. Yet it haunts us still.

The history of humanity is marked by a perennial desire to get back to the garden, that peaceful place where we live in God's presence. Perhaps that's why this botanical theme appears all over Scripture. Garden scenes make cameo appearances throughout the entire Bible from beginning to end.

As we've seen, God "planted" the first garden (Genesis 2:8). All other gardens producing harvests in season are themselves witnesses of God (Acts 14:17) and echoes of Eden. One of the first things Noah did to get settled into the post-flood world was to plant a garden (Genesis 9:20). This parallels God's preparation of the original creation in many ways. In these first two biblical gardens we see the themes of creation, loss, and human brokenness mingled with a hope of future redemption.

Adam and Noah both longed for beauty but ended up corrupting the very things they cultivated. Adam ignored God's words and lost paradise for himself and all his future descendants—like you and me. Noah gets drunk in his garden, in the shadow of the ark, providing an opportunity for his family to fall into grave sin, resulting in a curse on his grandson Canaan (Genesis 9). While we don't know much about this second garden episode, like the first, the results are devastating and generational—just read the book of Joshua and learn about Israel's military conquests in Canaan when entering the promised land. The sin in the garden affected both person and place.

Not every garden scene in Scripture is so terrifying. King Solomon valued pretty gardens (Ecclesiastes 2:5–6). His love letter to his young wife would lose all poetic power if robbed of its garden imagery. One is tempted, appropriately so, to read Song of Songs as being about more than mere human romance. I'm of the opinion this love letter points to a greater love, a divine love, which brings us back to a place of wholeness and restoration, back to a garden where we live with God.

God regularly uses garden language to talk about his love for his people. Look at God's song delivered through the prophet Isaiah:

> I will sing about the one I love,
> a song about my loved one's vineyard:
> The one I love had a vineyard
> on a very fertile hill.

He broke up the soil, cleared it of stones,
and planted it with the finest vines.
He built a tower in the middle of it
and even dug out a winepress there.
He expected it to yield good grapes,
but it yielded worthless grapes.

So now, residents of Jerusalem
and men of Judah,
please judge between me
and my vineyard.
What more could I have done for my vineyard
than I did?
Why, when I expected a yield of good grapes,
did it yield worthless grapes?
Now I will tell you
what I am about to do to my vineyard:
I will remove its hedge,
and it will be consumed;
I will tear down its wall,
and it will be trampled.
I will make it a wasteland.
It will not be pruned or weeded;
thorns and briers will grow up.
I will also give orders to the clouds
that rain should not fall on it.
For the vineyard of the LORD of Armies
is the house of Israel,
and the men of Judah,
the plant he delighted in.
He expected justice
but saw injustice;
he expected righteousness
but heard cries of despair. (Isaiah 5:1–7)

What follows in Isaiah is a devastating account of God's judgment on his people and the promised land in which they live. God allows the walls around his garden to be destroyed and his people to be exiled. But these garden passages don't leave us without hope. These fallen gardens set a dark backdrop for the blinding dawn of God's salvation. Just a couple chapters later in Isaiah, God promises to give the people a sign, a virgin who will conceive a child and his name will be Immanuel, "God with us." God's promised One will bring us back to God's presence!

Of course, we don't have to wait until the time of the prophet Isaiah to find this kind of hope in contrast to a fallen garden. In the darkest chapter of the Bible, Adam and Eve were told something very similar. Though Eve probably walked out of the first garden with a tear-stained face, there must have been a small flicker of hope in her eyes. One day a child would make it possible for humanity to again live with God.

So it shouldn't surprise us that the garden motif also shows up in the life of Jesus. He once told a story about a vineyard that serves as a summary for the biblical story of redemption.

> [Jesus] began to speak to them in parables: "A man planted a vineyard, put a fence around it, dug out a pit for a winepress, and built a watchtower. Then he leased it to tenant farmers and went away. At harvest time he sent a servant to the farmers to collect some of the fruit of the vineyard from them. But they took him, beat him, and sent him away empty-handed.
>
> Again he sent another servant to them, and they hit him on the head and treated him shamefully.

Then he sent another, and they killed that one. He also sent many others; some they beat, and others they killed. He still had one to send, a beloved son.

Finally he sent him to them, saying, 'They will respect my son.' But those tenant farmers said to one another, 'This is the heir. Come, let's kill him, and the inheritance will be ours.' So they seized him, killed him, and threw him out of the vineyard. What then will the owner of the vineyard do? He will come and kill the farmers and give the vineyard to others. Haven't you read this Scripture?

The stone that the builders rejected
has become the cornerstone.
This came about from the Lord
and is wonderful in our eyes?"

They were looking for a way to arrest him but feared the crowd because they knew he had spoken this parable against them. So they left him and went away. (Mark 12:1–12)

The language of the rejected stone becoming the cornerstone points back to Isaiah 28:16 and Psalm 118. Jesus is the son of the vineyard owner, who is rejected and killed. And he is the one who will conquer evil and lead us back into God's garden. Though rejected, Jesus is the most important stone, our rock of refuge (Psalm 18:2).

In the New Testament, you can often find Jesus in a garden. He prays in the garden of Gethsemane before his betrayal (Matthew 26:36–46). And after his crucifixion, he was buried in a garden tomb (John 19:41–42). It was in this garden that his followers first encounter him after the resurrection. The first on the scene was Mary Magdalene, a woman who had been demon-possessed before she had a life-transforming encounter with Jesus. Here's how John recounts that meeting:

> But Mary stood outside the tomb, crying. As she was crying, she stooped to look into the tomb. She saw two angels in white sitting where Jesus's body had been lying, one at the head and the other at the feet. They said to her, "Woman, why are you crying?"
>
> "Because they've taken away my Lord," she told them, "and I don't know where they've put him."
>
> Having said this, she turned around and saw Jesus standing there, but she did not know it was Jesus. "Woman," Jesus said to her, "why are you crying? Who is it that you're seeking?"
>
> Supposing he was the **gardener**, she replied, "Sir, if you've carried him away, tell me where you've put him, and I will take him away." (John 20:11–15)

It's no wonder Mary doesn't recognize Jesus when she turns around to respond to the voice of the one asking, "Why are you crying?" (John 20:14–15). Our own tears throughout the years answer the question as well. We've been seeking someone who can bring us back to a place of perfect peace. We're all just trying to get back.

Jesus is whom she was seeking. And behind all our attempts at security and joy apart from God, Jesus is whom we are seeking as well. We're looking for the Good Gardener.

If only Adam would have obeyed! If only he had protected his bride from the lies of the serpent! If only he had defended his turf! Could we have lived in that garden forever? Whatever you think of that question, it is powerful that the apostle Paul refers to Jesus as "the last Adam"

(1 Corinthians 15:45). Jesus came to do what Adam should have done in the first place. And Jesus gets the job done.

Jesus obeys the words of the Father, protects his bride, and defends his turf. And he promises to make the whole thing new, to lead us into a new garden where he will wipe the tears from our eyes, and where humanity will again live with God. Look at how the new creation is described:

> Then I saw a new heaven and a new earth, for the first heaven and the first earth had passed away, and the sea no longer existed. I also saw the Holy City, new Jerusalem, coming down out of heaven from God, prepared like a bride adorned for her husband. Then I heard a loud voice from the throne: Look! God's dwelling is with humanity, and He will live with them. They will be his people, and God himself will be with them and be their God. He will wipe away every tear from their eyes. Death will no longer exist; grief, crying, and pain will exist no longer, because the previous things have passed away. Then the One seated on the throne said, "Look! I am making everything new . . . . there will no longer be any curse." (Revelation 21:1–5; 22:3)

We see something interesting in the new creation that's similar to the original garden. We again see the Tree of Life (Revelation 22:2). There's much to consider here. Unlike the original creation, in the new creation there's no need for sun or moon, because Jesus is the light of the world. And, while we see a Tree of Life in this garden, there is no Tree of Knowledge of Good and Evil.

It seems we will no longer hunger for forbidden fruit. It appears it will no longer even be an option. We will gladly submit to the moral authority of our good King. Our exiled hearts will finally find a home. This is what awaits us: "Anyone who has an ear should listen to what the Spirit says to the churches. I will give the victor the right to eat from the tree of life, which is in God's paradise" (Revelation 2:17).

Praise God! What was lost in Eden will be restored. Because of Jesus, we can better understand this fallen world and our place in it. Better yet, we can cling to a promise that there's something beyond it, a place of peace and joy where we will again live with God.

Questions for Reflection

1. What do you think the Tree of Life symbolized?
2. What list of effects of the fall did you come up with from Genesis 3?
3. How does the promise of God making all things new encourage you?

The Stargazer's Song

*It is not the business of the church
to adapt Christ to men, but men to Christ.*
—DOROTHY SAYERS

There's no more harrowing question than the question of the self. There's no more costly line of thought than one's own identity. That's why it can be painful to look in the mirror—harder yet, to look into one's own soul. But we can't avoid ourselves forever.

Today it's not uncommon for those who hold a secular view of humanity to be blind to the limitations of their position. Their view of the world is simply too small. Their worldview is big enough for the world but not big enough for them. There's no room left for humans in their world. That's because when you reduce everything down to physical explanations, what gets left out is the human experience.

The philosopher Roger Scruton summed it up well when he asked, "Wait a minute: science is not the only way to pursue knowledge . . . Why not give weight to the disciplines that interpret the world and so help us to be at home in it?"[1] The disciplines he suggests for making sense of the human condition are ethics, art, and religion. Here, we're going to look at the religious perspective, in particular, the Christian view of humanity.

We've surveyed a lot of ground in this book, far more than we could adequately cover. We haven't had much time to linger. It's been more of a flyover than a close-up. I hope you'll go back and zoom in on doctrines we've introduced, so you can drill down deeper and work through Scripture to better formulate what you believe. Every theologian should explore the Bible for themselves in developing their own convictions. Theology is a lifelong process.

We've looked at how God communicates with his creation. We've considered the ways God has taught us to think about him. And it's all led us to this point, the point of facing ourselves. Instead of beginning our theology with our own experiences, we've started with God's revelation of himself. In light of what he's revealed about himself, we now turn our attention to making sense of the human experience.

In some ways, your human experience is unique. No one really understands what it feels like to be you. There's only one of you and your first-person perspective is just that, first-person. It's personal. It belongs to you alone. Yet, in other ways, we can all relate to the human condition, what it feels like to be human. But that raises the question, what exactly does it *mean* to be human?

A Living Masterpiece

God is an artist. And we are his art. The Bible says we are God's workmanship or masterpiece (Ephesians 2:10).

As an amateur artist, I know sometimes art needs a little context to make sense. An artist might have intentions and purposes that aren't self-evident to others.

Consider Impressionism. I really appreciate the work of the contemporary artist Makoto Fujimura. His stuff is amazing. But to fully appreciate his designs, you need some commentary of what he's seeking to convey—the message in his art.

Years ago, he was commissioned to create art to decorate the four Gospels. I treasured my oversized version of the first four books of the New Testament, illustrated with prints from this artwork. But when I went to hear him speak at an event in Chicago, I left with an even deeper appreciation for his work.

First, I was able to see the original art. It was much bigger than I expected, some pieces well over ten feet tall. His paints had substance and texture. Some included precious metals like silver and gold. Seeing the originals helped me better understand and appreciate my replicas.

Then Fujimura gave a talk about the inspiration for and theme of his work. He searched for a specific Scripture verse to serve as a motif for the project. After a lot of consideration, he landed on the only two-word verse in the New Testament: "Jesus wept" (John 11:35). He created his paintings to illustrate the Gospels, reading them through the tears of Jesus.

Now when I admire his final creations, I'm moved by this perspective. But without hearing him describe his intention, I never could have figured that out on my own. The art alone, even seeing it in person, wouldn't have given me all that.

The same is true for us. If we're God's masterpiece, as Paul explains, then we can only really know our purpose if our Creator makes his intentions known for us. That's what shapes our identity. We need God to explain who he created us to be. Like Fujimura's art, I might appreciate a lot about his work, but it's only when combined with his explanation that I can understand and interpret the art. The same is true for you and me.

A New Name

In biblical times, a person's given name was closely tied to their identity. Even in our day, names really are a big deal, aren't they? My parents named me Daniel after an Elton John song title. Impressive, I know. It's a good song, by the way. I like it a lot, which is a nice coincidence.

Throughout my life I've mostly been called other things, though. Some of them I won't put in print. For the most part they've been harmless nicknames. To this day, if I get a message for "Danny," I know it's someone from my hometown who knew me as a kid. You might have a nickname like that too. Sorry. I can relate.

Back when I served as a dean of a college in Kentucky, I vividly remember experiencing an existential crisis when my assistant came into my office and said someone asked if "Danny" was in. It's not that I minded a surprise visit from back home. It's that the visitor was someone, well, a teacher, whom, well, I got suspended for being, well, rather rude to. For full disclosure, I was in her class before I became a Christian, and my rudeness was also crudeness. But I won't get into the details. She and her husband had brought their college-aged son for a visit to our campus, and they decided to drop by the dean's office to say hello.

Long story short, we had a wonderful visit and even laughed about the incident that had happened so many years before. The memory of my past regretful decisions was triggered by my childhood nickname. Our names can have an awful or amazing effect on us.

In college I switched to Dan. That stuck. I can't get away from it now, though deep down, I prefer my full birth name. I certainly like it better than Danny. Daniel means "God is my judge." When you drop the "el" off my name, you're dropping off the part of my name that points to God. Elohim is a Hebrew name for God, and, often, the "el" at the end of a name is a reference to this.

That's one of the reasons I prefer it over nicknames I've been called over the years. You'll be able to tell if my publisher was willing to support my transition back to my full name by looking at the cover of this book. There's a lot that goes into a name.

When we experience a life-transforming encounter with Jesus, what we often refer to as conversion, we receive a lot of new titles. We are called "children of God" (John 1:12). We who were once enemies have become the "friends" of God (John 15:14). We are gloriously described as the "Bride of Christ" (Ephesians 5).

In addition to our new titles, we see that we will also receive a new name: "Let anyone who has ears to hear listen to what the Spirit says to the churches. . . . I will also give him a white stone, and on the stone a new name is inscribed that no one knows except the one who receives it" (Revelation 2:17).

An Excellent Name

As important as the name our parents gave us is, our identity doesn't begin there. It all starts with God, with *his* name, with him revealing himself to us. This is indeed the only way we can discover who we are.

In the Psalms we find the perennial question we've been discussing here: What does it mean to be human? It's asked by someone very familiar, King David. He's a guy with a checkered past. He had a lot to look back on, be thankful for, and be proud of. But did he ever have a lot of things to be ashamed of! I can't read anything by or about David without thinking about his complicated life. If David merely looked inside himself for answers, all he'd find is a convoluted mess.

The same is true for us. We can be tempted to define our identity by either our best days or our worst days. We can look to ourselves as a hero or a zero, depending on the day of the week. But in those moments when we become reflective, when we stop to think about life, perhaps when we, like David, look up to the night sky, we are tempted to dig a bit deeper. Who are we really, apart from our performance, apart from our good and bad days, or some average of the two?

That's a bit how this happened with David in Psalm 8. It's been called a "Stargazer's Song" because it only mentions the lesser lights, "the moon and the stars" (8:3). It's very different than Psalm 19 that we surveyed at the beginning of this book. Yet these two psalms serve as ideal bookends for our tour of the stream of orthodoxy.

Speaking of bookends, Psalm 8 has bookends of its own. It begins and ends with the same words, "LORD, our Lord, how magnificent is in your name throughout the earth" (Psalm 8:1, 9). As we've pointed out with other passages, here the first reference to "LORD" is in small caps. This is a reference to how God introduced himself to Moses, as Yahweh.

It all starts with a burning bush. You likely know the story. God calls Moses to do something amazing—to lead the nation of Israel out of Egyptian captivity. God tells Moses to go tell Pharaoh to let God's people go free. Moses, in his reluctance, asks God who he should say sent him. God responds by saying, "I AM" (Exodus 3:13–14). The English translation of the original Hebrew is "Yahweh," or "LORD" in small caps.

Back to Psalm 8. This song begins and ends with a clear emphasis on the God who reveals himself. This is the only way we can know God. I love how the British theologian J. S. Whale explains this: "there is no experience of God without a revelation of God. . . . Man asks questions about God to which revelation is the answer; but the answer is intelligible only because the questions are intelligible."[2]

This really sums up what we see going on in this Stargazer's Song. Smack dab in the middle of the psalm, David asks "What is a human?" This question makes perfect sense to someone looking up at the glistening stars created by the God who exists. But the answer only makes sense by listening to the God who has revealed himself. Apart from revelation, this question has no definitive answer. All of human history illustrates this point.

By stating the name of Yahweh, David shows us exactly where to look to solve the riddle of the human experience.

It's not to some generic God. The question is answered in the light of this God who speaks through a burning bush. The God who is. The God who speaks. The God who has spoken:

> Long ago God spoke to the fathers by the prophets at different times and in different ways. In these last days, he has spoken to us by his Son. God has appointed him heir of all things and made the universe through him. (Hebrews 1:1–2)

> Above all, you know this: No prophecy of Scripture comes from the prophet's own interpretation, because no prophecy ever came by the will of man; instead, men spoke from God as they were carried along by the Holy Spirit. (2 Peter 1:20–21)

> But as for you, continue in what you have learned and firmly believed. You know those who taught you, and you know that from infancy you have known the sacred Scriptures, which are able to give you wisdom for salvation through faith in Christ Jesus. All Scripture is inspired by God and is profitable for teaching, for rebuking, for correcting, for training in righteousness, so that the man of God may be complete, equipped for every good work. (2 Timothy 3:14–17)

In the past God spoke to prophets. He also revealed himself in history in the miraculous birth of Jesus, who was and is the Word of God. And the Spirit led the apostles to recall all Jesus had taught them. All this is preserved in Scripture for our benefit. If we are to know our purpose and identity, we have to look at what the Author of our story says about us. We are God's masterpiece, and he alone can explain our purpose and meaning.

More Than Animals

In contemplating human existence in light of the God who reveals himself, David's thoughts in Psalm 8 go back to the garden of Eden. David asks the question, "What is a human?" Then, for an answer, he turns to the opening pages of the Bible. David models for us where and how to look for our identity. In particular, we see how David is making sense of the human experience in light of what Genesis says about humanity's role in creation:

> You made him little less than God and crowned him with glory and honor. You made him ruler over the works of your hands; you put everything under his feet: all the sheep and oxen, as well as the animals in the wild, the birds of the sky, and the fish of the sea that pass through the currents of the seas. (Psalm 8:5–8)

> So God created man in his own image; he created him in the image of God; he created them male and female. God blessed them, and God said to them, "Be fruitful, multiply, fill the earth, and subdue it. Rule the fish of the sea, the birds of the sky, and every creature that crawls on the earth. (Genesis 1:27–28)

> God blessed Noah and his sons and said to them, "Be fruitful and multiply and fill the earth. The fear and terror of you will be in every living creature on the earth, every bird of the sky, every creature that

crawls on the ground, and all the fish of the sea. They are placed under your authority. Every creature that lives and moves will be food for you; as I gave the green plants, I have given you everything. . . . But you, be fruitful and multiply; spread out over the earth and multiply on it." (Genesis 9:1–4, 7)

When God created Adam and Eve, he gave them authority in the world (Genesis 1:28). In many ways, they were like the king and queen of Eden. They ruled the world. But they were to rule over nature under God's authority. They were, as David says, less than God, but more valuable than everything else. This theme is repeated to Noah after the flood, as you can see in Genesis 9, above. Part of the answer to what it means to be human is seen in the differences between humans and the rest of creation.

God defines our identity as above the rest of creation. However else we define humanity, if we let Scripture set the parameters for us, we must draw a clear distinction between animal life and human life. Look at how Jesus teaches the disciples to think about this question:

Don't fear those who kill the body but are not able to kill the soul; rather, fear him who is able to destroy both soul and body in hell. Aren't two sparrows sold for a penny? Yet not one of them falls to the ground without your Father's consent. But even the hairs of your head have all been counted. So don't be afraid; you are worth more than many sparrows. (Matthew 10:28–31)

This passage highlights another distinction between humans and animals. Jesus explains humans have both a soul and a body. The Bible often uses the term *spirit* for soul as well. To be human is to be both body and soul. Jesus repeats this distinction elsewhere, like when he told the disciples the "spirit is willing" but the "flesh is weak" (Matthew 26:41). The apostle Paul teaches a distinction between body and soul when he describes death as being absent from the body but present with the Lord (2 Corinthians 5:8).

Being human means to be both body and soul. You can see this in what Jesus describes as the greatest commandment, to love the Lord with all our heart, soul, mind, and strength (Mark 12:30). This command is so difficult to follow, as we discussed in the last chapter, since humanity is now fallen and under the curse of sin. So how does this affect our view of what it means to be created in the image of God? Do we still bear God's image?

Personal Reflections

To answer that, we first need to consider what's really going on in the text of Genesis when it says God made Adam and Eve in his own image. There are a couple of different Hebrew terms for the word *image*, and both refer to something similar, but not identical, to whatever the image resembles. Adam and Eve, as beings created in the image of God, are like their Creator in certain ways. But how? In what ways do humans resemble the Creator?

Since God isn't made out of stuff, he has no physical properties. He is immaterial, so there is no reason to think Adam and Eve somehow looked like God in a physical way. The image language must mean something other than appearance. To get at answers to our questions, I'll summarize four different ways to think about the doctrine called *imago dei*, a Latin expression meaning "image of God."

Humanity reflects God in how they can rule

The first view of the *imago dei* focuses on how humans were created to *rule*. As we've seen, it's clear that humans are meant to have dominion on the earth (Genesis 1:28). That's an obvious function of humans in the passages we've looked at in Genesis and even in Psalm 8. We could say more about what it means to be in God's image, but, on this view, the image language itself is about dominion or ruling.

Humanity reflects God in how they can relate

The second perspective of the *imago dei* emphasizes how humans have the ability to *relate*. Genesis shows us how Adam and Eve have a unique relationship with God in comparison to the rest of creation. To be in God's image speaks to the ability of humans to relate to their Creator.

Like the first view, there is clear evidence for this distinction in the text. Instead of focusing on humanity's rule over creation, this view emphasizes humanity's ability, in contrast to everything else in creation, to have an intimate relationship with God. As Genesis indicates, God "walks" only with humans. He relates to Adam and Eve differently than he relates to the rest of his creation.

Humanity reflects God in how they can reason

The third way of seeing the *imago dei* is to focus on humanity's ability to *reason*. This position seeks to unpack the ways that humanity is substantively different from the rest of creation, often with an emphasis on rational capacity. Many theologians will detail a number of ways humans have greater capacity than animals: they have greater intellect, artistry, language, and the like. For example, the contemporary theologian and author Wayne Grudem outlines fifteen ways humans are substantively different from other creatures.[3] While many scholars would argue that "intellect" is not what's meant by the image language in Genesis, I don't know any who would dispute there are real differences in capacity between humans and animals.

Humanity reflects God in who they are

A final way of understanding humanity as God's image-bearers focuses on what we *are*. This is sometimes called the ontological view. *Ontology* is a word that means essence or being. Instead of making the image language about humanity's ability to rule, relate, or reason, this position places the emphasis on human nature. This position is not about what a human has or does, but what a human is.

The benefit of this option is that it guards against ways the doctrine of humanity could be misapplied. For example, a person could lose their abilities to rule, relate, or reason. A person could have physical, social, emotional, or mental limitations or disabilities. Would that mean they are no longer image-bearers? As a friend of mine likes to point out when he teaches on this topic, the first three views are easily hijacked. If we make the *imago dei* somehow tied to human capacity, what a person *can* do, then what if that capacity is diminished? What if they can no longer do those things?

Surely, theologians holding any of the other positions we've mentioned would want to place our worth as image-bearers somewhere deeper than human ability or capacity as well. Why? Because our worth is found in our very nature. We are made in the image of our Maker. And that means we have intrinsic worth not based on anything we do, but entirely on who we are, as those made in God's image.

Since the biblical texts about being created in God's image are not explicitly clear in terms of the full range of meaning implied by the expression "image of God," I find all of the positions helpful in different ways. Yet I think the priority needs to be given to the intrinsic worth of humanity best communicated through the *ontological* view. Consider, for example, the Old Testament basis for capital punishment, what we refer to as the death penalty: "And I will require a penalty for your lifeblood; I will require it from any animal and from any human; if someone murders a fellow human, I will require that person's life. Whoever sheds human blood, by humans his blood will be shed, for God made humans in his image" (Genesis 9:5–6).

Murder is punishable by death, not because of the loss of a human's ability to rule, relate, or reason. It's because of the significance of humans as made in God's image. The clear emphasis here is on the intrinsic value of image-bearers, apart from anything they are able to do.

Theologian Millard Erickson expresses this value when he says, "[The *imago dei*] refers to something a human *is* rather than something a human *has* or *does*. By virtue of being human, one is in the image of God; it is not dependent upon the presence of anything else."[4]

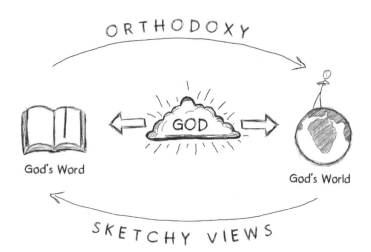

Intrinsic Worth

While I was in graduate school, I remember the day someone put racist propaganda on my friend's car at church. We
were both parked in the side lot, and when we came out of
the service together, we saw a bright flier on his car. I was
parked nearby, but there was no flier stuck under my windshield wiper like his. We wondered if his car was chosen,
not mine, because of his license plate. I still had Illinois tags
on my car. His Jeep had Georgia tags. We speculated that
someone might have thought he'd be more receptive to the
racist message since he was from the South. To be clear, he
was not receptive. Both of us were angered by the hateful
message and its proximity to our place of worship.

The divide between South and North is a reminder of
the importance of this doctrine. This dividing line has separated a nation, families, and even churches. Sadly, it was a
reality my friend and I couldn't escape even at our religious
graduate school, the Southern Baptist Theological Seminary. And I'm not just referring to the propaganda on his
windshield.

Southern Seminary was founded in 1859, a year before
the Civil War broke out. It was the flagship school for a
denomination that took its name, *Southern Baptist*, after
splitting from Baptists in the North who opposed owning
other people as property. The first president of the seminary
was James P. Boyce, a known racist who supported slavery.
Why would Christians tolerate such evil views?

The answer is in part because of a misunderstanding
and misapplication of Scripture. But even this understates
the point. The real reason is because of wickedness and
sin. The world may think someone is less of an image-
bearer (or not one at all) because of their skin color,
language, or socioeconomic status, and then can justify

treating them differently. But we can't justify those beliefs from Scripture.

As I write this, I'm sitting in a town in Ohio, where the racist Ku Klux Klan (KKK) once saved Martin Luther King, Jr.'s life. It sounds crazy, I know. But it's true.

In 1965 Martin Luther King, Jr., was speaking at Antioch College in Yellow Springs, Ohio, the school from which his wife graduated years before. There was an assassination attempt planned, with about ten shooters who intended to open fire on King and the audience during the ceremony. But at the last minute, a Klan rally was organized in the nearby city of Lebanon, Ohio, on the same day. The mob decided to attend the Klan gathering, instead of completing their assassination plans.[5]

King, who was indeed assassinated a few years later, is best remembered for his sacrificial civil rights work and his famous "I Have a Dream" speech. If you were to read his speeches, you'd find a common theme about the shared humanity of all people as created in the image of God.

The biblical doctrine of the *imago dei* provides an exclusive foundation for intrinsic human value, equality, and dignity. Even the language of America's Declaration of Independence isn't able to capture or protect human rights. "We hold these truths to be self-evident, that all men are created equal." Sounds good, but we know all too well that equality isn't always common or self-evident. Sometimes the most evident thing about us is how we discriminate and take advantage of those unlike us.

The mere fact these claims were made by a nation that benefited from the African slave trade makes it clear human equality isn't self-evident. Was it self-evident that Native Americans were equal? I don't raise these questions to become unnecessarily controversial, but to stress the importance of properly understanding that humans are created in God's image. This is a doctrine with real-life and real-time implications. It means a world of difference for everyone in the world. And if the doctrine of the *imago dei* is true, as I of course believe it is, then Christians should be the first and loudest voices to speak against prejudice and for human equality.

Amazing Grace

Like pretty much all of America, where I live in Ohio is filled with history related to the unfortunate ways humans get this wrong. This area of the country was very active in helping slaves from the South migrate north in search of freedom. The national museum for the Underground Railroad is not far away in Cincinnati. Enslaved men and women seeking freedom would travel in the darkness of night and rest during the day at homes of friendly supporters.

My neighbor's house is officially registered as having been a part of the Underground Railroad. It's likely our house, which was built in the 1800s, was once active as well. When doing a significant renovation project, the previous owner discovered a hidden room in the basement with no doors or windows. The only way to access this secret room was by removing a board in the master bedroom closet on the first floor. There's still a rickety, old stepladder down there that I would imagine people used to get in and out. Visitors to our home often want to check it out for themselves. I once had my theology class over for a meal, and about fifteen of my students crammed into the space for a quick photo op.

About four miles from my house is the nation's first historically Black college and university, named after William Wilberforce. Wilberforce was a British parliamentarian who fought to end slavery. His pastor encouraged him in his work. Before becoming a Christian, his pastor had been a captain of a slave ship. His name was John Newton.

Newton once wrote a poem called "Faith's Review and Expectation," reflecting on the kindness of God in saving someone who had contributed to such an evil practice as buying and selling humans as property. Over the years, the words to that poem were set to music and a new title was adopted.

"Amazing grace, how sweet the sound, that saved a wretch like me," Newton wrote.[6] Newton and Wilberforce worked with numerous others to put an end to the slave trade in the British colonies. It's estimated that the song "Amazing Grace" is performed over ten million times per year. It is arguably the most recognizable song in human history.

If we try to discover human equality and intrinsic worth in something that seems self-evident to us, sadly we will always find someone who sees things differently. If we look within ourselves to find our worth, we will surely end up in despair. If we look around us, to our culture, we will find pressing questions with no lasting answers. But if we want to know who we are, we need to look to the God who has revealed himself. We need to look to Yahweh.

Instead of placing human value at the level of what is self-evident to humans, the Bible places our worth in the revelation of God. It is in the radiance of the burning bush, when God revealed himself to Moses, where we find our great opportunity to know the value of a human soul. Like King David says in Psalm 8, it is in the name of Yahweh, the God who reveals himself, where we can find an answer to the inescapable question, "What is a human?" And in the shadow of the cross of Christ we learn the true value of the human soul, that God loved the world so much, loved *us* so much, he gave and didn't spare his own son (John 3:16, Romans 8:32).

Questions for Reflection

1. Why is it important to consider what a human is in the light of the name God revealed for himself?
2. What difference should the Christian view of humanity make on how we live and treat others?
3. What are some practical ways you can apply the doctrine of *imago dei* in your own life in the next week?

The Mouth of the River

*All human nature vigorously resists grace
because grace changes us and the change is painful.*
—FLANNERY O'CONNOR

In the spring of 1940, one of the first female graduates from Oxford University delivered a prophetic speech about the evils of Hitler's Nazi regime. Germany had just invaded Poland months before. They would soon begin bombing England. Author and novelist Dorothy Sayers warned the British people of the real reason the world conflict was coming to their front door. It had nothing to do with being naughty, she told her audience. Instead, Hitler was doing what he believed was right. Sayers explained that he was playing by a different rule book.

Sayers explained the problem was that people had become bored with doctrine. She used the word *dogma*, which is another word for theology. The fundamental clash between Hitler and the rest of the world was due to differing theologies. The growing war, she explained, was a result of, "a violent and irreconcilable quarrel about the nature of God and the nature of man and the ultimate nature of the universe."[1] It's not that Hitler was breaking a rule he believed in and knowingly committing a sin. Instead, he was being obedient to a very different rule, which he accepted as absolute, true, and good. His didn't see his war as a crime but a conviction.

In this way, Hitler's campaign was based on *bad* theology. He didn't properly understand the world or his place in it. He got God wrong, and everything else too. Sayers pointed out the sad reality that people weren't thinking deeply enough about the difference between Hitler's convictions and their own. They weren't able to recognize sketchy views of God when they saw them.

Begin with God

Here's the point. If you get God wrong, you'll get a lot of other stuff wrong too. I'm not saying you'll commit war crimes like Hitler. That's not what I mean. I know plenty of people with very different views than mine, even atheists, who are very kind and responsible persons. What I do mean is if you don't properly understand God, you'll never really understand yourself or the world in which you live.

That's why it's so important to begin with God's revelation of himself. This is why the Proverbs tell us the fear of God is the beginning of wisdom (Proverbs 9:1). As we've discussed throughout the book, the stream of orthodoxy flows from this fountainhead. We make sense of our world by beginning with the Maker of our world and what he's told us about himself.

Of all the Scriptures we've looked at so far, two psalms provide bookends for everything we've talked about. They summarize the banks of the river of orthodoxy. The first is Psalm 19, with its focus on the excellence of God's Word in making sense of the world. The second is Psalm 8, with its central question of what it means to be human. These psalms frame our quest to make sense of God's Word, God's world, and our place in it.

The title of Sayers's speech was "Creed or Chaos." Her point was that there's not a neutral position. We will have a creed, or we will have chaos. We will have a good theology or a sketchy one. But none of us is living in this world without some view of God, without some kind of theology that affects the way we see everything else.

If we choose ignorance or laziness, we're really choosing chaos. If we want to make sense of reality, Sayers argued, we have to adopt a creed based on God's revelation of himself. If we want to make sense of God's world, we have to begin with God's Word. If we want to push back the chaos, we have to understand and embrace the creed.

The stream of orthodoxy is flowing through the land of God's two books: God's world and God's Word. God has revealed himself in nature, and he has revealed himself in Scripture. Both books have to be interpreted. The book of nature is fallen. The book of Scripture is infallible. So to make sense of God's work in the world, we have to begin with God's Word. Orthodoxy flows in this direction.

It's creed or chaos.

If we make our own experience the authority, we will likely get God wrong. Instead, we should interpret our experience in light of who God is. And we know who God is by looking at what God has revealed about himself. This is the Christian elephant. We believe God exists, is personal, and has revealed himself.

It's this or it's nothing. It's creed or it's chaos. This is the flow of orthodoxy. This is the path to life.

Our Compass in the Wild: A Quick Recap

There can be all kinds of things Christians disagree about, but our source of authority should be our foundation for unity. God's revelation of himself is the baseline. We might interpret the Bible wrong, the world wrong, or we might interpret them both wrong. (We're pretty clever at getting things wrong it seems.)

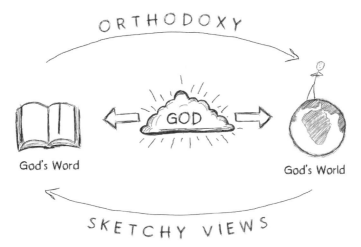

We can't, however, let our imperfection lead us to ignore what God has said about himself. That's where we begin, and that's where we return. That's our only hope. That's the source of our creed.

The Bible gives precious little space to what the world was like before the fall. The same is true regarding details about the new world to come. Most of the Bible is about life outside of the garden of Eden, in the wilderness of this life. Most of the Bible is about the in-between. The Bible provides a road map for finding a flourishing faith in this fallen world.

It all begins with God. The first step to making sense of God is to recognize he's there, and he's not silent. This changes everything. Orthodoxy begins by recognizing God has given us parameters for how to think about him. He's also told us how to talk about him. He's the author and owner of it all. The choice is ours to respond to his moral authority or not. But we don't have the proper credentials to define God however we want. That's pretty apparent in the opening pages of the Bible when our forefathers lost paradise.

Pastor and author John Stott once said, "The Word of God is the scepter by which Christ rules the church."[2] It's in God's revelation of himself that we find answers to our recurring human questions. Our best efforts, apart from God's revelation, end in heartbreak.

God's Word is inspired. God is its author. God Word is inerrant. He used human authors to write what he wanted without error. God's Word is infallible. It's a reflection of God's own character. Because God is perfect and cannot lie, we have confidence in his Word.

God is also the source of our material universe. He exists outside of time, space, matter, and energy. In God's explanation of himself, we find the mysterious reality of God as a perfect unity in the midst of diversity. God is Father, Son, and Spirit. Each person of the Trinity is fully God. Yet there is only one God. Scripture frames this beautiful portrait of the one God who made all that exists.

The oneness of God sets the parameters for what we believe about God. God exists by himself. He is dependent on nothing or no one. He is one. He exists without parts, passions, or potential. He is faithful. He is unchanging. We can trust him.

The world God created in its original state was good. Because of Adam and Eve's disobedience, we are in a world scarred by their sin and infected by our own sin. But the Bible points us to a new creation, where, through the ministry of Jesus, all things will be made new. The Bible gives us a guide for how to faithfully live in this fallen world, while we fix our eyes on Jesus, the author and perfecter of our faith. This is the Christian story and hope in a nutshell.

A Final Fishing Story

I went kayaking the other day on the Stillwater River here in Ohio. As far as fishing goes, I had a pretty good day. I can't complain. I caught several smallmouth bass. But the view and the scenery were the most amazing thing about the experience. Nature has always been therapeutic for me. And as I said earlier, it always turns my thoughts toward God.

I put my kayak in the water downstream and then worked my way up to the point where the current was too strong to go any further. That's my preferred way to fish. I work hard in the morning to make it upstream and then float and fish on my way downstream in the afternoon. As the day wore on, I docked my kayak and walked along the shoreline. I stood at the bend in the river where some rapids were so loud you could barely hear anything else. It was amazing.

Theology can be like this at times. There are moments when we stand in the solitude of truth and reflect on God's goodness. Then there are times when truths about God absolutely overwhelm us. We're left speechless, standing in awe. I'm not sure which I prefer more. Both are remarkable.

It's my prayer that this short book will provide a helpful introduction to a lifelong journey of exploring the stream of orthodoxy. We've really just hit a few highlights related to some key doctrines about God, God's Word, and God's world. There's so much more to explore. I'm reminded of the passage in C. S. Lewis's closing story about Narnia called *The Last Battle*. Lewis ends the saga with the children entering the new creation. Check it out:

> All their life in this world and all their adventures in Narnia had only been the cover and the title page: now at last they were beginning Chapter One of the Great Story, which no one on earth has read: which goes on for ever: in which every chapter is better than the one before.[3]

No matter how much you study the Bible, you'll never exhaust the knowledge of God. There will always be more. Even when we enter eternity, when any false beliefs we've formed in this life will surely be left behind, we will still not know everything about God. We'll spend eternity in ever-increasing awe of who God is and all he has done.

I remember a well-intentioned Sunday school teacher telling me that when we get to heaven, we will know everything, just like God. I don't find that anywhere in the Bible. Paul tells us, "in the coming ages he might display the immeasurable riches of his grace through his kindness to us in Christ Jesus" (Ephesians 2:7). We will spend eternity learning more and more about God's grace. Every second of eternity will be a "wow" moment.

As I mentioned at the beginning of the book, it's important to have a method for how you think about God. Start with the main thing. Interpret the confusing things in light of the clear things. Mind the boundaries. Don't travel alone. And last, but not least—enjoy the ride!

My prayer for you is the same as my prayer for the theology students I teach at the university. I pray you will never get over God and his Word. I pray you will frame your beliefs of God from Scripture, so you avoid sketchy views. I pray you will understand who you are and your place in the world as a response to what God has revealed in the Bible. Always ask—what does faithfulness to the text require?

Last of all, I pray the Lord blesses you and causes his face to shine upon you and gives you peace. This is my prayer for you all. Amen.

Endnotes

Chapter 1: A Stream Called Orthodoxy

1. A. W. Tozer, *The Knowledge of the Holy: The Attributes of God. Their Meaning in the Christian Life* (New York: Harper & Row, 1961), 9.

2. Alister McGrath, *Heresy: A History of Defending the Truth* (New York: HarperOne, 2010), 33.

3. Gilbert Keith Chesterton, *Orthodoxy* (London, England: The Bodley Head, 1908), 85.

4. E. Randolph Richards and Brandon J. O'Brien, *Misreading Scripture with Western Eyes: Removing Cultural Blinders to Better Understand the Bible* (Downers Grove, IL: IVP Books, 2012), 12.

5. Peter Kreeft and Ronald K. Tacelli, *Handbook of Christian Apologetics* (Downers Grove, IL: IVP Books, 1994), 98.

6. Stephen William Hawking, *The Illustrated Brief History of Time,* 2nd ed. (New York: Bantam, 1996), 233.

7. Philip Schaff, *History of the Christian Church*, vol. 7 (Grand Rapids: Eerdmans, 1965), 650–653.

8. My list is inspired by the helpful theological method outlined in Michael F. Bird, *Evangelical Theology: A Biblical and Systematic Introduction* (Grand Rapids: Zondervan Academic, 2013, 2020), 92–93.

Chapter 2: Chasing Elephants

1. James Sire, *Naming the Elephant: Worldview as Concept* (Downers Grove, IL: IVP Academic, 2015), 15–16. I've adapted this illustration slightly, replacing the kangaroo with a giraffe. I'm not sure why I've done this. I just like the giraffe better, I suppose.

2. Crispin Sartwell, "Irrational Atheism," *The Atlantic,* October 11, 2014, http://www.theatlantic.com/national/archive/2014/10/a-leap-of-atheist-faith/381353.

3. C. S. Lewis, "They Asked for A Paper," in *Is Theology Poetry* (London: Geoffrey Bless, 1962), 164–165.

4. Mark Foreman, *Prelude to Philosophy: An Introduction for Christians* (Downers Grove, IL: IVP Academic, 2013), 44.

5. Oscar Levy, ed., *The Complete Works of Friedrich Nietzsche: Beyond Good and Evil*, trans. Helen Zimmern (Edinburgh, England: T. N. Fouis, 1914), 34.

6. Bertrand Russell, *Religion and Science,* 2nd rev. ed. (Oxford: Oxford University Press, 1997), 255.

7. Alex Rosenberg, *The Atheist's Guide to Reality: Enjoying Life without Illusions* (New York: Norton, 2011), 18.

8. J. S. Whale, *Christian Doctrine* (London: Cambridge University Press, 1956), 19, 27.

9. C. S. Lewis, *Reflections on the Psalms* (New York: Harcourt, Brace, and World, 1958), 63.

10. Michael Licona, *The Resurrection of Jesus: A New Historiographical Approach* (Downers Grove, IL: IVP Academic, 2010), 229.

11. Norman Geisler, *Systematic Theology*, vol. 1 (Grand Rapids: Bethany House, 2002), 253.

Chapter 3: Three Divine Eyes

1. See Bruce Metzger, *The Early Versions of the New Testament: Their Origin, Transmission, and Limitations* (Oxford: Oxford University Press, 1977).

2. R. C. Sproul, *What is Faith?* (Orlando, FL: Reformation Trust Publishing, 2010), 4–7.

Chapter 4: Oh, the Humanity!

1. Norman Geisler, *Systematic Theology*, vol. 1 (Grand Rapids: Bethany House, 2002), 524–525.

2. Geisler, *Systematic Theology*, 533.

Chapter 5: What's the Matter?

1. See Robert Jastrow, *God and the Astronomers* (New York: Norton, 1978), 16.

2. Arno Penzias, "Clues to the Universe's Origin Expected," interview by Malcolm Browne, *New York Times,* March 12, 1978.

3. William Lane Craig, *The Kalām Cosmological Argument* (Eugene, OR: Wipf and Stock, 2000). Also, see the helpful video describing this argument produced from Craig's writing: https://www.reasonablefaith.org/kalam.

4. *Aladdin*, produced by Walt Disney Feature Animation, 1992.

5. Brian Vickers, ed., *Francis Bacon: The Major Works* (Oxford, England: Oxford University Press, 2008), 371–372.

6. C. S. Lewis, *The Seeing Eye*, from *Christian Reflections*, ed. Walter Hooper (Grand Rapids, MI: Wm. B. Eerdmans Publishing Co., 1995), 167–171.

Chapter 6: Saint Patrick on Making Sense of God

1. I'm certain I've heard something like this example before, but I can't for the life of me remember where. I pass it on with the hope it might help you recognize there is nothing new under the sun. Like the author of Hebrews, I'm tempted to merely state, "Somewhere it is written." If you're reading this and you're the one who first originated this illustration, way to go. This endnote is in your honor.

2. This argument shows up in several of C. S. Lewis's essays and books. Most notably, Lewis refined and defended his formulation of this argument in his book *Miracles* (London: Geoffrey Bles, 1947).

3. See a helpful overview of philosophy in R. C. Sproul, *The Consequences of Ideas: Understanding the Concepts That Shaped Our World* (Wheaton, IL: Crossway Books, 2009).

Chapter 7: The Ocean in a Teacup

1. William Lane Craig, "The Doctrine of God (Part 1)," *Defenders*, podcast audio, May 7, 2007. https://www.reasonablefaith.org/podcasts/defenders-podcast-series-1/s1-introduction/the-doctrine-of-god-part-.

2. James E. Dolezal, *All That Is God: Evangelical Theology and the Challenge of Classical Christian Theism* (Grand Rapids: Reformation Heritage Books, 2017), 20.

3. Hilbrook Jackson and Gilbert Keith Chesterton, *Platitudes in the Making: Precepts and Advices for Gentlefolk.* (Ignatius Press, 1997), 25.

4. Gerald Bray, *The Attributes of God: An Introduction* (Wheaton, IL: Crossway Books, 2021), 26

5. Bray, *The Attributes of God*, 27.

6. Norman Geisler, *Systematic Theology*, vol. 2 (Grand Rapids: Bethany House, 2003), 47.

Chapter 8: Mere Creation

1. Francis Schaeffer, *Genesis in Space and Time* (Downer's Grove, IL: IVP Press, 1972), 57.

2. Dietrich Bonhoeffer, *Dietrich Bonhoeffer Works, Volume Three, Creation and Fall: A Theological Exposition of Genesis 1–3* (Minneapolis, MN: Fortress Press, 1997), 28.

3. John Lennox, *Seven Days That Divide the World* (Grand Rapids: Zondervan, 2011).

4. J. P. Moreland et al., eds., *Theistic Evolution: A Scientific, Philosophical, and Theological Critique* (Wheaton, IL: Crossway Books, 2017).

5. *Karate Kid*, directed by John G. Avildsen (Colombia Pictures, 1984).

Chapter 9: Our World Fallen

1. Daniel DeWitt, *Life in the Wild: Fighting for Faith in a Fallen World* (The Good Book Company, 2016).

2. Nels F. S. Ferré, *Evil and the Christian Faith* (New York: Harper and Brothers Publishers, 1947), ix.

3. Richard Dawkins, *River Out of Eden: A Darwinian View of Life* (New York: Basic Books, 1995), 133.

4. Alex Rosenberg, *The Atheist's Guide to Reality: Enjoying Life without Illusions* (New York: Norton, 2011), 18.

5. Dietrich Bonhoeffer, *Dietrich Bonhoeffer Works, Volume Three, Creation and Fall: A Theological Exposition of Genesis 1–3* (Minneapolis, MN: Fortress Press, 1997), 28.

6. C. S. Lewis, *Mere Christianity* (New York: Macmillan, 1952), 53–54.

Chapter 10: The Stargazer's Song

1. Roger Scruton, *On Human Nature* (Princeton, New Jersey: Princeton University Press, 2017), 12.

2. J. S. Whale, *Christian Doctrine* (London: Cambridge University Press, 1956), 29.

3. Wayne Grudem, *Systematic Theology* (Grand Rapids, MI: InterVarsity Press, 1994), 442–450.

4. Millard Erickson, *Christian Theology*, 2nd ed. (Grand Rapids: Baker Books, 1998), 532. Emphasis in original.

5. Lisa Powell, "Did you know Martin Luther King Jr. was targeted for assassination at local college commencement?" *Dayton Daily News*. January 15, 2021, https://www.daytondailynews.com/news/local/the-plot-assassinate-mlk-during-visit-yellow-springs-was-called-off-due-disorganization/UFN8lLXADML8DBPVubCMJL/.

6. John Newton, *Olney Hymns, in Three Books,* 5th ed. (London: J. Buckland and J. Johns, 1788). Book I, no. 41, p. 43.

Chapter 11: The Mouth of the River

1. Dorothy Sayers, *Creed or Chaos?* (New York: Harcourt, Brace, 1949), 29

2. John Stott, *Between Two Worlds: The Challenge of Preaching Today* (Grand Rapids, MI: William B. Eerdmans Publishing Company), 1, 78.

3. C. S. Lewis, *The Chronicles of Narnia: The Last Battle* (New York: HarperCollins, 2001), 767.